"*Rick Broniec, through his heart felt journey of healing ...
will inspire and guide you to move forward with your own.*"
Wendy L. Darling, founder of Miraculous Loving, Author of The Miracle That Is Your Life

THE SEVEN
GENERATIONS
STORY

An Incentive for Healing Yourself,
Your Family and the Planet

RICK BRONIEC, MEd

The Seven Generations Story:
An Incentive for Healing Yourself, Your Family and the Planet

By Rick Broniec, MEd.

Cover Design by Melodye Hunter
Typesetting: Zonoiko Arafat

ISBN: 978-0-9961446-5-0 (p)
ISBN: 978-0-9961446-6-7 (e)

Crescendo Publishing, LLC
300 Carlsbad Village Drive
Ste. 108A, #443
Carlsbad, California 92008-2999

www.CrescendoPublishing.com
GetPublished@CrescendoPublishing.com

A Message from the Author

Rick Broniec, MEd.

https://vimeo.com/121518771

To help you implement the strategies mentioned in this book easily and get the most value out of the content, I've prepared the following bonus materials I know you'll love:

- Exercise Guide
- Video Teachings

Even if you decide you may not be ready for *The Seven Generations Story* yet or that it just isn't for you, please accept these special gifts just for stopping by and checking it out:

- A Guide for Writing Powerful and Effective Goals
- "Body Scan Mediation" Audio for healing your own body at the cellular level

You can get instant access these complimentary materials at:

http://www.SevenGenerationsStory.com/

Dedication

I thankfully dedicate this book to my parents, William C. and Beverly I. Broniec. I also dedicate it to my daughters, Heather M., Erica L. and Gianninne B. N. I also dedicate this book to my precious granddaughters: Skye Sunshine, Jaida LaRue, and Kienna. You have all inspired and loved me unconditionally. And I sincerely hope you have benefitted from my healing work!

Keep on Healing!

love,

Rich

Table of Contents

How to Use This Book

I created this book to be used as a guide through your journey. It is my hope that you experience transformation, acceptance, and deep personal growth.

To assist you in attaining the best possible results, I have included some interactive materials and access to additional bonus content to continue your progress.

Each chapter includes exercises intended to help you reflect and discover as well as video teachings from my own Seven Generations Story keynote.

Foreword

If you were to see a picture of me, at first glance you might think I am a man of European ancestry, and you'd be mostly right! My last name is Polish. It was Americanized when my great-grandparents emigrated here from Poland, but originally it had a "z" at the end. "Broniecz" means "warrior" in Polish, by the way! However, I am also part German, French, Irish, Scottish, and Cherokee Indian. Obviously, I appear European, and I wasn't raised on a reservation as a Native American man, yet that Native American part of my heritage is very important and precious to me. One thing I discovered from exploring my Native American heritage is that many of my Aboriginal brothers and sisters share a common but powerful belief that when a person heals him or herself, that healing extends to seven generations—in both directions! I've heard that many times in a Native elder's prayers and sacred ceremonies. So I learned that when I do some healing work on myself, it will effect my father's generation and my grandfather's generation backwards as well as my children's generation, my grandchildren's generation, forwards and so on into the future. Isn't that a wonderful belief? Think about it: my healing and growth somehow magically extends backwards and forwards to heal seven generations of my family—and perhaps other families. Is it possible that I can actually change my family's long legacy of dysfunction, mental illness, and substance abuse just by doing my own healing?

Do you find that a comforting image? I know I do—that I can actually change my family's generational story by doing my healing and personal growth work. Wow! What a wonderful and unexpected bonus for having the courage to dive into my own healing work! And doesn't that belief make my own healing that much more urgent, worthwhile, poignant, and important? I want to share with you in this introduction, and throughout this book, some stories of my own family and my own healing that might just illustrate this amazing phenomenon to you more clearly.

At the age of thirty-seven, I was a national award-winning and highly respected high school chemistry teacher in Racine, Wisconsin, just south of Milwaukee. I was very good at it and loved my work, but somehow, at that stage in my life, it didn't seem very fulfilling. I was also a father of two precious young daughters, a husband, a church member, a lay minister, a brother to five siblings, a son, and a grandson. Despite all of this apparent richness in my life, I was feeling very lost, empty, sad, and strangely alone. My marriage was in deep trouble. My well-cultured persona of competence and positivity, hidden behind a perpetually smiling face, was beginning to crumble despite my desperate efforts to maintain the fiction that "everything is all right" and "I'm totally in control" to the world.

Eventually, marriage issues and stress drove me (kicking and screaming, believe me!) into what would become a lifetime exploration of my own story and my own healing. I dove into therapy, many healing workshops, some "Twelve Step" work, and intense men's circles in a deep way that continues to this day—and that will continue for the rest of my life. The story of my awakening and healing is a good one, one that I freely share later in this book, but that is not the focus of this introduction.

What I do want to share about my healing here is that I began to reclaim many parts of myself that I had been cut off from—my feelings, my authenticity, my purpose and mission, and my passion, just to name a few. As I reclaimed those parts of myself, I began to heal. I began to re-script the stories that were deeply ingrained in my psyche about who I was, what my role in life was, and what I was supposed to do. I began to understand that much of these messages were coming from old family wounds that were passed on to me. And, most important for this introduction, I began to see how I was passing on to my beautiful daughters these very same negative messages! I found myself doing and saying the exact same things that I vowed I would never do or say to my children! How many of you have had that experience? I sincerely doubt that I'm the only one!

Now back to my story. After several years of therapy and group work, I was ready, in March 1990, to do a powerful men's training called The New Warrior

Training Adventure (NWTA). Put on by a men's organization called the ManKind Project (mkp.org), the training claimed to be initiatory in nature. I was told I would be initiated into healthy male energy and invited to reclaim pride in my maleness. I was also told I would find my Mission of Service for my life and would be strongly supported in removing any blocks that lived in me, that were stopping me from living my Mission fully. It worked beautifully! That training profoundly changed my life! I was truly initiated into a powerful new way of being. I joined an ongoing men's group that came out of my NWTA, and I am still in that group some twenty-five years later! It has taken all of those twenty-five years to fully integrate the learning I received from my NWTA!

Soon after my NWTA, I became aware of a deep, uniquely male wound I carried, a wound that writer and men's work icon, Robert Bly, christened "the Father Wound." So many men carry this wound. For most of us, it comes from not having close, authentic, emotionally bonded relationships with our fathers, or not knowing our fathers at all. I learned early on that my father wound was quite different from most men. I DID have a close, loving relationship with my dad. In fact, he was a very loving man and hugged and kissed all six of his kids regularly; he often told us how much he loved us and how very proud of us he was. We were very blessed in that way. Even so, my father wound, though different, went just as deep as most men's did. You see, my dad was a wildly successful salesman. He approached the world with a persona of outgoing happiness and a "can do" attitude. He always smiled and almost always had good things to say about people. That was his nature; he was a "glass half-full" kind of man. So, what was my wound? It took awhile, but I finally figured it out: I needed to hear my father's failures, his mistakes, his regrets, and his difficulties. In living behind his façade of positivity and "successful salesman," I missed hearing of his struggles and regrets. And, of course, I was just like him in that way! I carried more of my father than just his name!

I realized that I needed to have a talk with my dad one on one—and soon. So I approached him at Christmas that year and said, "Dad, I'd like to spend some time with you. Would you be available for that?" He replied, "Sure, Rick. Let's get your brothers up here, and we'll go fishing together." I replied, "No Dad, just you and me." And I let it drop.

We were together again at Easter, and I stated my request again. He replied, "Great! Let's me and you and your wife and kids go camping together next month." I said, "No, Dad, just you and me." Do you see a pattern here? He KNEW I was somehow emotionally changed after my NWTA and the other work I was doing and that I wanted something from him. He knew that I was hungry for a part of my father that he didn't want to share, or didn't know how to share. It scared the heck out of him, I realized. So, I let it go again. But the need did not go away in me; in fact, it intensified as I continued the hard and painful work of peeling back my own façade so that I could become more authentic and more emotionally available, so that I could show my daughters, my wife, my friends, and my family my own tears, my fears, and my failures.

Fast-forward a couple more months. Out of the blue, I got this call from my father, "Hi Rick, how would you like to go fishing with me up north in September? Just you and me?" I smiled broadly, then replied, "Great idea, Dad! I can't wait!" It took nine long months for him to decide to spend this time with me! And now it was finally happening.

We—just the two of us—spent four glorious and moving days together camping at a remote lake in northern Wisconsin. We got up at sunrise each morning, fished all day, and then cooked our catch and talked around the campfire as we ate our dinners. We talked long into the night. What happened during those four days was magical and healing. I believe that my own work and my capacity to really listen to my father allowed him to begin to open up emotionally to me in a way that I'd never experienced before. He reminisced about the tragedies in his life and his regrets. He shared stories that I had never heard before. We cried together more than once.

I had known, for example, that my father's father had died when my dad was only fourteen years old. What I did not know were the profound consequences of losing his father at such an early age just before the end of the Great Depression and the beginning of World War II. Like me, my father was the oldest son of his family. I learned he had to forgo his plans to go to college in order to go to work—first part-time and then full-time—to help support his mother and younger brother. What I also did not know was his deep, lifelong grief at losing his life's dream: to become a professional musician and to teach music in schools. You see, my father was a gifted musician. He *loved* music; he could pick up virtually any instrument and within minutes would be playing it like he had played it all his life. Music clearly was his passion and his love—especially clarinet music like the kind the Benny Goodman orchestra played at the ballrooms my father frequented in Chicago in the 1940s. In fact, my parents met at a Benny Goodman concert in Chicago in1949, when they had their first date and first dance together.

I also knew that times were very tough for him and his family, as they were for so many in those post–Depression days. My dad found he had a talent for sales and dove into that as a way to support his family. He worked very hard at sales and became quite successful for the next fifty years, even though it was not his real passion. At the time of our fishing trip together, he had just retired, which meant he quit his full-time job but kept working his three part-time jobs! (Did I say my father was a workaholic?) And the first thing he did after "retirement"? He joined the community marching band in his small town of Adams, Wisconsin. Just that summer, in 1991, I had the extreme joy of watching my father march down Main Street tootling "Yankee Doodle Dandy" and "God Bless America" on his clarinet in the Fourth of July Parade!

He was in his glory! His smile was a mile wide as he passed us on the curb. What a terrific memory.

Now, back to our camping trip. On our last night together, my father must have felt safe enough and loved enough and heard enough to share a story he had never shared with anyone before. He told me that at his father's funeral, his Uncle John* had come to his mother and said, "With your husband gone, you can't take care of Billy (my father's nickname). Why don't I take him to my house and I'll take care of him for you." His mother, no doubt in shock, agreed. Then my father turned to me in a very matter-of-fact manner and said, "And that night was the first time my uncle had sex with me. This went on for about two years until my mom could afford to bring me home. She never knew."

Needless to say, I was stunned. I immediately burst into tears. In my deep empathy and compassion for my father's pain, I reached out for his hand and held it tightly. "Dad," I croaked, "how did you survive that abuse? What did you do with this experience all these years?" He replied, "Rick, I did with the memories what everyone of my generation did with their awful experiences. I stuffed them deep down inside and never talked of them again. I have not even shared this story with your mother or my mother, and I ask you not to share it with anyone while I am alive. But somehow, I knew I had to share this with you tonight. I am so very relieved at finally telling someone!" That amazing night, I had the incredibly moving opportunity of cradling my father in my arms as he sobbed out this painful story for the very first time. I simply listened and held him through this process. I have tears in my eyes now as I write about that surreal, moving, and unforgettable night.

Somehow, we made it through that evening. It brought us closer than I could have imagined. I felt such love and respect for my father... and such profound sadness that he had carried these terrible experiences and memories for so long. And I felt his love and respect like never before—and also his deep trust in me that allowed him to share such a painful and intimate story. I was amazed once again at my father's beautiful humanity.

At some point that night, I asked my dad to consider doing the ManKind Project training I had done so that he could get the same healing benefits I had experienced. He said he'd let me know after he thought about it for a while.

The next morning, as we packed to leave, my dad said to me, "Rick, thanks so much for last night. I feel so much lighter now that I have finally shared this secret! I have carried that pain and shame for a long time, but I let go of much of it around the campfire last night, thanks to you, son. I am very grateful." What a huge gift!

Just two weeks after our fishing trip, I received a handwritten letter from my dad that I still have today. In it he thanked me for sharing the precious time we had together. He honored me for the obvious emotional healing work I had done on myself, for the openness I shared with him so freely and the man and father and teacher I was becoming. He noted how good he had felt coming home from that trip, and then he wrote, "Even so, I don't think I could do the work you're doing in your life, Rick. I think it's just too difficult to dredge up those old painful memories—and I know at some level I have to do that to heal completely. I am so proud of you for doing this for yourself, as well as for your family. But I am going to decline your kind offer to do the ManKind Project weekend. Honestly, I'm just too old to dredge up those painful memories that have been buried for so long." Periodically, I unfold that letter and read it again and have a good cry with my father. I miss him so very much!

As I write this part of my story, I am tearful, once again, at my keyboard, for my father's words were prophetic. Just three months later, on the day after Christmas 1991, my beloved father died unexpectedly. Perhaps it will be no surprise to you that my dad died of heart failure. His heart literally broke, I believe, from years of holding in this painful story.

Now take a deep breath, my friends. Let's move on, but I promise you, I'll come back to my father's story! There's a beautiful postscript.

I call my youngest daughter, Heather, my shame-free daughter. She was just about a year old when her mother and I began to do some deep inner healing work. I am convinced that by doing my work around my shame and my masks and my unconscious family roles and so much more, I was able to father my daughter in a different way than I was raised. And the results of that healthier parenting soon became apparent.

For example, when Heather was young and she did something like spill a glass of milk, she would simply say to her mother and me, "It's OK. I just spilled some milk. I'll get a towel and clean it up!" And she did so with a smile on her face and absolutely no sign of shame or self-blame for the spill. And NO drama! Can you imagine being that free of shame when you were just three years old? Can you imagine reassuring the adults in your life that everything would be OK? It took my breath away back then, and it still does today!

Now fast-forward twenty-four years. I have raised my two daughters and my stepdaughter. I now have three precious granddaughters. (We don't do boys in my family! I wonder why I was attracted to men's work!) They are now ten, six, and four years old. Oh my God, are they beautiful, precious, and wonderful! You grandparents reading this know exactly what I mean, right?

A while ago, I was on the phone with Heather's oldest daughter, Jaida. She was just four and a half years old then, and she was babbling excitedly like only a four-year-old can. She was joyful and energized and precocious and so excited to talk to Grandpa that I really could understand only every other word. And you know what? It didn't matter one bit! I was so deeply touched by her energy and exuberance and passion for life that my heart was overflowing with love and joy. I stopped her after a time, and I said to her, "Jaida, do you know how precious you are to Grandpa?" She was quiet for just a very short moment and then replied in her high and energetic voice, "Yes, Grandpa, I am amazing!" Wow! Can you imagine confidently proclaiming that you were amazing to the big people in your life—and meaning it—when you were only four years old … or, for that matter, ever? Does anybody reading this remember doing that when you were small (and surviving!)? I simply cannot imagine it! I would have been smacked down hard by my parents, or grandparents, or uncles, for daring to speak out loud the sentiments that I was special, or smart, or even a good person. I would have been sternly reminded, "You think you are so special? Well, you're not!" and "Who do you think you are?" How many of you heard similar messages early in your life? The vast majority of us have heard such messages, right?

So in our short time together, you already know enough about me to know what happened next, right? Of course! I immediately burst into tears—this time tears of joy. The tears literally shot out of my eyes. This was undoubtedly one of those magical moments when I was just grateful to be alive!

And in that moment, my friends, I had a flash of clarity, a gestalt, that brought me instantly back to the "Seven Generations story" I started with and that is the theme of this book. I realized that my joy was the result of realizing and really "getting" the impact of my twenty-five years of healing work on my family. The entire history of the Broniec family was changing right before my very eyes. It was, and is, a miracle! I am smiling broadly now as I write these words. I believe that my own deep work had a healing effect on my father that invited and allowed him to share his deepest secrets. I believe my personal growth work also affected my daughter in a good way, too. She was now passing that healthy-ness on to my granddaughters! And I can imagine it being passed to my great-granddaughters, as well. Think about it! It is truly a miracle. Generations of familial shame and blame were disappearing like magic! And all I had to do was face my own demons first. All I had to do was my own healing and personal growth work—nothing more.

In that flash, I came to know that my wise Native American brothers and sisters were right. My healing work was also healing seven generations of my family—in both directions. Whether you are Native American or not, whether you ascribe to that belief or not, I lovingly and gently invite you to go on your own healing adventure. Read on for some more examples and lots of support. Then I invite you to dip your toe into the deep end of the "healing pool," or, if you're ready, dive in deeply with me! And if you are already on that path, please, please continue. The world is waiting for us. And it is time.

Perhaps your family is also waiting for it, maybe even depending on it. Generations in both directions, I suspect, are hoping and praying for it. I believe the whole planet is waiting expectantly. And I know you can do this, my friends; if I can do this, anyone can! I truly believe that my wonderful granddaughter Jaida articulated a great and universal truth that day on the phone: Not only is she amazing, you are, too. You are *all* amazing—every last one of you! You are beautiful and precious and you have much to offer the world. I believe that to my core! Moreover, you deserve it; you deserve to believe in, enjoy, and completely own your goodness and power and beauty.

I sincerely believe this story holds much hope and promise for you and your family, for mine, and, in fact, for the whole world! I hope you believe this and embrace it, too!

*Please note: The names and some identifying details were changed in the stories in this book to protect the privacy of people involved. All stories are shared with permission of the participants.

Chapter 1

The Seven Generations Story – What Are Its Origins?

"As we live our lives preparing the road for the Seventh Generation, let us not forget that we are the Seventh Generation for those that came before us … honor those Relations, consider and protect their teachings and be thankful that, because of them, we have these things we hold close to our hearts. … We are the Seventh Generation!"
Tim Blueflint

"In every deliberation, we must consider the impact of our decisions on the next seven generations."
Iroquois Proverb

"The Seventh Generation Principle today is generally referred to in regards to decisions being made about our energy, water, and natural resources, ensuring those decisions are sustainable for seven generations in the future. But it also can be applied to relationships—every decision should result in sustainable relationships seven generations in the future."
Bob Joseph, "Working Effectively with Aboriginal People" Blog

What is some of the history around this powerful Seven Generations story? How did this story become so important to Native American mythology over the years? Where did it come from and what is its purpose? Let's explore these questions. Native American writer Tim Blueflint traces the story back to the Algonquin People of the northeastern US. On his website, he states, "It has been repeated not only in the oral tradition of the People, but is widely recognized in all forms of media today and takes a personal meaning to many individuals. As I see it, the core of the Seventh Generation teachings is the intent that each should consider the effects of their actions and lives on each future generation ... to the seventh generation in the future." Blueflint goes on to say, "Today it is our responsibility to prepare the way for future generations by honoring the past; embracing, protecting and teaching what is remembered to our children." [1]

Despite Blueflint's assertions, however, most writers and historians believe this story or principle dates to the Iroquois nation. This perspective is shared by Iroquois Elder, Oren R. Lyons, who said, "The Seventh Generation is about Vision; it's about leadership looking ahead, it's about responsibility. Seven Generations reminds you that you have responsibility for the generations that are coming seven generations ahead, or over 150 years from now. And that indeed you are in charge of Life as it is at the moment. People in the United States have the Bill of Rights, they always talk about their Rights but not about their Responsibility." Elder Lyons reminds us eloquently of our responsibility to care for future generations. He goes on to state, "Leadership has got to have that [responsibility for seven generations into the future] above all, they have got to have vision, they have got to have compassion for the future, they have got to make decisions for the seventh generation. That is not just a casual term, [sic] that is a real instruction for survival."

In fact, the majority of writers and historians trace the Seven Generations story to the laws and agreements created by the Iroquois Confederacy. The principle dates back to "The Great Law of Iroquois Confederacy," which was written sometime between 1142 and 1500 AD, long before Europeans had fully colonized US soil! The Great Law of Iroquois Confederacy formed the political, ceremonial, and social fabric of the Five Nation Confederacy (later a Sixth Nation was added). Of note is the strongly held conjecture that The Great Law of the Iroquois Confederacy is also credited as being a contributing influence on the American Constitution, due to Benjamin Franklin's great respect for the Iroquois system of government.

"The Seventh Generation Principle today is generally referred to in regards to decisions being made about our energy, water, and natural resources, But it can also be applied to relationships—every decision should result in sustainable relationships seven generations into the future."[2] This quote is compelling testimony to the historical and ecological significance of the Seven Generations principle/story, as well as how relationships can benefit from it. Imagine ... our US Constitution is, in large part, based on the Great Law of the Iroquois Confederacy, as is much of our environmental awareness, yet few US citizens really know or understand the true significance of this story, or how it relates to our own well-being and healing. Fewer still understand how this story can affect our families' history and healing.

The ecological significance of the Seven Generations story is better known and often referred to by both Native and non–Native people as an incentive for caring more carefully for Mother Earth. There's even a thriving company called "Seven Generations,"™ based in Burlington, Vermont, that produces ecologically sound products like cleaners, detergents, and paper products![3] Less well known is the connection between the Seven Generations story and how it relates to relationships, especially with regards to generations up to 175 years into the future!

Grandmother Rita Blumenstein of The International Council of 13 Indigenous Grandmothers points out the familial healing aspects of this story when she states, "The past is not a burden, [sic] it is a scaffold which brought us to this day. We are free to be who we are— to create our own life out of our past and out of the present. We are our ancestors. *When we can heal ourselves, we also heal our ancestors, our grandmothers, our grandfathers and our children.* When we heal ourselves, we heal Mother Earth."[4] Grandmother Rita states so clearly how the Seven Generation story connects our own healing to that of our family lineage as well as to the healing of our planet. Powerful words, indeed!

Grandmother Rita, along with twelve of her compatriots and allies, is highlighted in the award-winning documentary *For the Next Seven Generations*.[5] I encourage you to view this wonderful, powerful film to see how these thirteen committed grandmothers rallied together to travel throughout the world in an effort to remind our modern world of the significance of our own healing and awareness, as well as that of our families. It is a delightful, moving film, well worth the time and effort.

So far, I have traced the history of the Seven Generations story (or principle) back to its Native American roots. We've seen how this story relates to the historical record, the ecology movement, and to the concept of caring for our Earth and for the seven generations that follow. I'd like to go on to make a stronger case for the concept of healing generational pain and familial stories for *seven generations in both directions*. From Quoteland.com: "If you heal something, you've healed seven generations back and seven forward." What else is written about this concept that is perhaps difficult to understand?

Let's continue with words from Sister Jose Hobday: "The concept of the Fourteen Generations remains one of the most broadening and challenging. The idea seems simple—deceptively so: you pay reverence and respect to the seven generations that have gone before you and the seven generations that will come after you.

According to this tradition, you keep seven generations, forward and back, in your mind and heart in everything you do, and live accordingly."[6] Sister Hobday shares the "challenging" belief that what we do affects seven generations in both directions from us—fourteen generations in total. It may seem clearer to us that what we do and how we heal will filter down to our children, our grandchildren, and so forth into the future. It may even make sense that we can influence our parents and grandparents. What may seem less obvious is how we can influence and help heal generations who have long since died. Yet this is exactly what Sister Hobday is stating so clearly!

Further strong support for this idea comes from Dr. Judith Rich in her article published in the *Huffington Post* in 2011 entitled "Healing the Wounds of Your Ancestors"[7]: "Some Native Americans believe that our actions affect the seven generations in both directions. Think about that possibility. Is it possible that we can evolve our lineage backwards in time as well as forwards? Does it matter? And why bother? Isn't that ancient history? Maybe not. Consider not only that it's possible to evolve your lineage in both directions, but also that to have this awareness cuts to the core of the true nature of human being. We're here in a body, appearing to be separate. We appear to lead separate lives, to have different experiences, beliefs and opinions about what is true and right and how the world works. This is true—at the level of appearances." How does this work? How can our lineage be healed into the past?

Dr. Rich goes on to explain: "As you step to the front of the line in your ancestry, the energy they embodied has been passed on and is now expressing as you and those of your current generation in the lineage. As you transform, the energy of the entire lineage preceding you is transformed, for it is all happening now through you, as you. You are the one who can heal old wounds for your entire lineage, forgive old enemies, shift conditioning and beliefs, release pain that has held preceding generations captive for centuries.

"This is the gift you bring them, for as they departed, they left behind the residue of their unfinished business, passed down through the ages, held in place by the unspoken family agreement to perpetuate it— that is, up until now. And now it's your turn. Bringing completion to prior generations and setting up what happens for future generations now depends on you.

"You can take this as a burden and decline to answer the call. This is how the wound keeps reproducing itself. Or you can see this as a gift and an honor, an opportunity to contribute to those you'll never see or know, those who may never know your name. And you can choose to do the work of healing yourself and them." Wow, what inspiring words Dr. Rich has shared! And I strongly resonate with her writing. I believe, and have ample anecdotal evidence to support, that what I do impacts my family generationally into the past and future. This is truly a revolutionary and powerful belief that calls us all to "do our own healing work."

For example, Dr. Rich says, "Perhaps you come from a lineage of addiction, from people who found solace and comfort from what seemed unbearable through alcohol or other substances. You might come from a lineage of anger or violence, from people who kept score and settled them in ways that were destructive to themselves and others. Maybe your people tried hard to assimilate and fit in, but never quite succeeded, always the 'outsider.' Maybe you still feel that 'outsider-ness' in your own life today. Your people might have been survivors, having lived through war or other atrocities. Many fought the battles, inner and outer, with those conflicts having been passed on to you."

These words speak to me deeply. Do they have meaning for you? Do you believe, as Dr. Rich and I do, that your actions, your healing, even your thoughts can affect your family lineage and the world into the past and future? Do you believe your DNA code can actually be rewritten through your own inner work? Do you accept the challenge to heal yourself so that your family line can also be healed—knowing that this will bless all the generations that follow you—AND preceded you? These are big questions!

I have accepted this very challenge. As I've shared in my introduction, I have actually witnessed the changes that have miraculously appeared in my father, daughters, and granddaughters as a direct result of my own work—my own commitment to my emotional and spiritual growth and awareness. I will share more stories of this miracle as we proceed! But first, I'd like to share more of Judith Rich's words because they resonate so deeply with me:

"Our 'job' here is to be the light that we already are and reflect that light outward so that others might find their own way in the darkness. The wounds we carry dim the light. As we do the work of transforming our wounds into gifts that help to bring about healing, we literally begin to shine. We become radiant beings who reflect their true nature, which is luminosity. Or, as Carl Sagan said, 'We're made of star stuff.' We are light beings as much as the stars.

"It takes courage to do the work of healing. It's not comfortable, convenient or easy. It's not 'business as usual,' or maintaining the status quo. It means the end of denial, pretending and avoiding. It means being radically honest with yourself and those around you. This kind of honesty won't necessarily win popularity contests, but it will recalibrate your DNA.

"If we're healing and transforming the wounds we carry from those who came before, we're also changing the trajectory of those who come after. Those who follow will have a different standard as the foundation for the lineage. If we break the chain of addiction, violence or other inherited, limiting beliefs, our children and their children and those who follow them are given access to possibilities not available to the ancestors. And thus, the entire lineage evolves." Thank you, Dr. Rich, for so clearly and passionately stating a great truth I believe to the depth of my soul! I believe that the philosopher's stone, so ardently sought by mystics and alchemists during the Middle Ages, was not about changing actual lead metal into gold, but rather was all about changing the "lead" of our wounds into the "gold" of our fully realized selves. How beautiful and poignant to know that my work today will give opportunities to the generations who follow (AND who preceded me) to access possibilities not even dreamed of!

So there's the challenge clearly stated! We can choose to dive deeply into our own healing, to reclaim our own light and the very real truth of who we are, OR we can shrink back, deny our power to heal ourselves and our lineage, and go back to sleep.

Perhaps the poet, Rumi, was speaking of this very concept in this wonderful poem:

> **Don't Go Back to Sleep**
>
> **The breezes at dawn have secrets to tell you.**
>
> **Don't go back to sleep!**
>
> **You must ask for what you really want.**
>
> **Don't go back to sleep!**
>
> **People are going back and forth**
>
> **Across the doorsill where two worlds touch,**
>
> **The door is round and open.**
>
> **Don't go back to sleep!**
>
> **Rumi**

The choice is ours. The choice is clear. The doorway is

round and open. We can work to break our own "chains of addiction, violence and other inherited, limiting beliefs" and thereby change our own story and our collective DNA and that of seven generations in both directions. We can choose to be "radically honest" with ourselves, and our loved ones. We can consciously and purposefully choose to "transform our wounds into gifts" and radiate our light powerfully to the world and truly claim the luminosity that is our (and our family's) birthright. Or we can "decline to answer the call and allow our familial wounds to continue to perpetuate themselves." We can "go back to sleep."

What will be your choice?

http://www.SevenGenerationsStory.com/

Chapter 1 Exercises

Exercise 1: In the space below, capture your key family stories. Catalog your familial history of abuse, violence, suicide, murder, sexual abuse or rape, financial mistakes, alcoholism and other substance abuse, and so forth. Be radically honest. If you're not certain about a particular part of the story, please interview some of your living relatives to glean some of their truth. Then journal what these family stories and behaviors have cost you. What parts of you have you allowed to shut down? What limiting beliefs about yourself have you unconsciously taken on? What possibilities may have passed you by?

Exercise 2: In the space below, now capture some of your family gifts. These are passed down, too! What talents, abilities, and positive behaviors were passed down to you? How have you been blessed by your family system? Detail how that has affected your life.

Exercise 3: What personal growth or spiritual work have you done to address the issues raised in your answers to Exercise 1? What do you think you still need to work on to change the story and limiting beliefs that resulted from them? How will you do that work? Who will support you?

Exercise 4: Now take an important moment to acknowledge yourself for the progress already accomplished! Allow yourself to feel great about the changes you have already introduced into your family system. Then write a couple commitments for continued growth. Be specific: What will you do? By when? Who will assist you? How will you know when that phase is complete? How will that feel? Go to my website www.SevenGenerationsStory.com to get a free guide for writing clear and powerful goals.

Exercise 5: I invite you to write a couple affirmations to use on a daily basis to spur your personal work. Keep affirmations in the positive, in the present tense, and be specific. For example: I am a loving and forgiving man. Or: I release all limitations to attaining financial prosperity. Post your affirmations around your house or car, anyplace where you will see them—and repeat them—often each day! Go to my website www.SevenGenerationsStory.com to get a free guide for writing wonderful and empowering affirmations.

Chapter 2

What Is My Personal Connection to The Seven Generations Story?

"You are a link in a chain of causation that stretches before and after your life for a thousand generations."
Chris Michaels, Founding Minister of the Center for Spiritual Living

"This is the true joy in life, the being used for a purpose recognized by yourself as a mighty one; the being a force of nature instead of a feverish, selfish little clod of ailments and grievances complaining that the world will not devote itself to making you happy. … Life is no 'brief candle' for me. It is a sort of splendid torch which I have got hold of for the moment and I want to make it burn as brightly as possible before handing it on to future generations."
Oscar Wilde

DNA carries ancestral patterns: not just physical characteristics like blue eyes, but also traits & tendencies such as your grandpa's bad temper or your mother's patience.
James E. Talmadge

My Native American Heritage

I am certain the Seven Generations story would not

have impacted my life nearly as profoundly if I did not have some Native blood in me—and valued that part of myself. How I came to know of this part of my heritage is an interesting story in itself.

When I was twenty-one years old, I was home from college for the summer and my mom and I were looking at some old family pictures. I saw an old black-and-white picture I'd never seen before of a tall man (about six feet two) and a very short woman (maybe four feet ten) who was obviously a Native American woman dressed in buckskin and a headband. Both people in the picture looked well worn and unhappy. On its back, the picture was dated 1870. I asked my mom who that was in the picture. She reluctantly replied, "Oh, that is your great-grandfather Neal … and his wife. She was a full-blooded Cherokee woman whom he married while in Oklahoma. They had ten boys, one of whom was your grandfather, Guy Neal." I was completely stunned! I had not been told that there was Native American blood in me! That important fact had never even been hinted at! I was also angry that this secret had been kept from me for twenty-one years. I asked my mother why this family history had been kept secret, and she stated that there was much family shame about having Native American blood, and that this was a stigma that was heightened by the rampant and open racism of that era.

In addition, my grandfather was a prominent preacher and hands-on healer in Zion, Illinois (a church-run city north of Chicago). He would have lost his church ministry and been ostracized if it had become known that he was half-Indian, so that secret was buried deeply. This story became one of those family secrets that no one talked about. (My experience is that most families have such secrets!) My mom still felt bound by that shame, even in 1973! As a result, I did not find out until I was a senior in college that I was one-eighth Cherokee! I wasn't sure how to feel about this fact. It took several years for this information to sink in and for me to fully integrate it into my sense of self.

A few years later, I began to explore and consciously reclaim my Native heritage. I had always been attracted to Native American mythology and ceremony—now I knew why! Then a bit later—in the mid-1970s—I became really hungry to learn more about that part of my heritage. So I read many books about Cherokee and other tribal history, attended a native encampment in the Nevada desert (run by a well-known Medicine Man, Rolling Thunder) for part of a summer, participated in Native ceremonies and sweat lodges, went to workshops with Native Shamans, and attended many pow-wows and celebrations. I purchased some authentic Cherokee items on a trip to Oklahoma and displayed them in my home. I made an elk-skin drum and learned to play it well, and I took some lessons on a Native flute. I found all of this learning to be very grounding. It felt like I was reclaiming an important part of my story that I had previously been denied. In a real sense, I felt like I was coming home.

Though I didn't live as a Native man, the one-eighth

portion of my DNA that was Cherokee became a very important and cherished part of my identity. And that's when I started to become aware of the Seven Generations story. I had read about this ethic forty years ago, but it really hit home and touched me deeply when I heard Native Elders and Shamans talk about the mystery and power of this story. I soon learned much of what I shared in Chapter 1 about the story and its origins and importance to many Native tribes. Now, I'd like to share a little more about my background and why I was so strongly called to my own healing path. (This next section is reproduced from my book *A Passionate Life: 7 Steps for Reclaiming Your Passion, Purpose and Joy.*[8])

"I was born in February 1952, in Chicago, Illinois, to a Polish, German, Irish, French, Cherokee Catholic family. I am named after my father and paternal grandfather. I am the oldest son of the oldest son of an oldest son. I have five wonderful siblings, two brothers and three sisters. I also enjoy having twelve nieces and nephews as well as three spectacular granddaughters!

"In 1959, when I was seven years old, an event happened in my family that colored my worldview for many years. My parents separated (for the first of seven times!). I remember that day as clearly as if it were yesterday. It is seared into my memory. I remember my father putting me on his knee and telling me that we weren't going to be living together anymore. He encouraged me to be strong, to support my mother and my brothers and sisters, and to 'become the man of the family.' And then he left.

"To this day, I am absolutely convinced that my father was trying to bless me and lovingly shield me from the effects of this breakup. I have no doubt that he was attempting to show me his love in the best way he could. At the same time, I am very aware of what a curse his words became for me—for many, many years of my life!

"The next day, my mother moved me and my siblings out of our suburban, middle-class home into a tenement house in the central city of Milwaukee, Wisconsin. We left the Catholic Church and joined a church of Yoga, which in 1959 was considered to be beyond radical. I became a vegetarian. I went from practicing prayer to learning meditation. I went from studying the Bible to reading the *Autobiography of a Yogi*. I went from my all-white, private Catholic grade school to an inner-city, mostly African American public school—overnight! My siblings and I were displaced, separated from everything we knew, and I felt really, really lost. And my mother, who tried her best to be there for us, was also struggling with her pain, loss, and confusion about what had happened to her marriage and her relationship to her church and her God.

"What had the most impact on me, however, was that my father's words went directly to my heart and soul, and I instantly began to live as if I was the 'man of the family.' I unconsciously made a powerful choice that day. I deeply internalized what my father's words meant for me and began to implement that message as best as my seven-year-old mind and heart could. I did this out of deep love and loyalty to my parents. I did this out of loving concern for my siblings and my mother. I did this earnestly and assiduously.

"In retrospect, it's easier for me to see all the effects of that choice I made that fateful day in 1959. Essentially, I became an adult that day. I lost my childhood, a big part of my aliveness, my playfulness, and my passion. I became my mother's surrogate husband and protector. I became my siblings 'second father,' which was exacerbated by the fact that I was left 'in charge' of my siblings often as my mother went to work to help support us. It took a long time for my siblings to forgive me for the damage I did to them in that role. I became super responsible and strongly focused on achievement and looking good to the world. I became deeply unconscious of my faults and unwilling to admit to them and my needs. My emotions were put under wraps almost immediately. I became what author and speaker John Bradshaw calls a 'Human Doing' instead of a 'Human Being.' And I thought this was 'just the way I am'!

"Fast-forward thirty years to 1988. By that time, I had graduated summa cum laude from college, earned my master's degree in chemical education, been married to my first wife for seven years, had two beautiful young daughters, owned a home, had a very successful career as a science educator, and had been a volunteer lay minister and board member in my church for eighteen years. I had won numerous national and state teaching awards, including the Presidential Award for Excellence in Science Teaching in 1987. I had also been a published author and had created and lead dozens of workshops for teachers at state and national conventions and had created and presented numerous seminars on cutting-edge science educational issues. I worked on the side as an educational consultant for IBM and the State of Wisconsin Department of Public Instruction. I was very well known and highly respected in my field.

Beginnings of My Waking Up

"By all outward appearances, I was wildly successful and living a good, productive life as a husband, father, teacher, and minister. On the inside, however, a very different story was unfolding. I felt unfulfilled, frustrated, and hollow. I did not know how to express my feelings in productive ways, and I felt like I was not really alive. My marriage was in deep trouble. Our love life was in a shambles. I felt like a fake, an imposter who did not deserve all the 'good stuff' I was experiencing. I smiled all the time and appeared well adjusted and happy, while inside I was filled with angst, resentment, self-doubt, and fear. Even my spiritual work, years of daily meditation and leading several services at my church each week, had little meaning to me. I was a workaholic and I was miserable. I lived behind a carefully crafted mask of perfection and invincibility. I taught, parented, and ministered out of a sense of duty, rather than from a deep well of energy and calling. I had virtually no passion for life!

"Somehow I knew that something had to change. My wife and I had been in psychotherapy for years, but the attention had been mostly placed on her, as a sex-abuse survivor. The message I got from these sessions was, 'You're all right, Rick. You are coping well. It's your wife that needs therapy.' Part of me was delighted to 'get a pass' from doing any real work on me, and part of me knew that I had to change significantly if my life was to have any meaning. So my wife and I went to a new therapist, Laurie Ingraham, in Milwaukee. She put us into her thirteen-week program of learning about being an 'adult child of a dysfunctional family' called 'The Ingraham Process' (TIP). That process, and the ongoing support group that met twice a week, was a big turning point in my life. There I learned about family systems and about the role I, and my siblings, had been unconsciously playing since early childhood. There I began to discover the reality of who I was. I began the painful process of peeling off the mask I had worn so well and so deeply. I began to learn some simple, yet powerful communication techniques that bless me to this day. I started to do my own work … and to become more alive!

"I discovered John Bradshaw at the same time and, through his writings and workshops and Laurie's teaching, became clear about my 'Family Hero' role—a role that my family so desperately needed me to play. As the oldest son, I was thrust into this role without my consent or understanding. I was the straight 'A' student, the sports star, and the minister who gave my family a public persona of success and proud accomplishment. I became the rock on which everyone else counted to be strong and grounded. Most everyone looked up to me while I had no one to trust or share my feelings and needs with. I was isolated and scared, and I coped by becoming sadly and caustically sarcastic.

How Doing Work in the ManKind Project™ Accelerated My Growth

"Soon after this first awakening through my TIP work, I was invited to do a men's weekend retreat near Milwaukee, Wisconsin, called the 'New Warrior Training Adventure' (NWTA), in March of 1990. This training, put on by a small, budding men's organization called the New Warrior Network (today this organization has become international and is known as The ManKind Project or MKP—check it out at mkp.org)[8] that had started in Milwaukee in 1985. One fact that attracted me to do the NWTA was that there were more volunteer staff on the weekend than there were participants (or 'initiates,' as we were called)! I figured (correctly) that any program that attracted so many men to staff again and again had to have great value. The staff men had a strong sense of purpose: to give back to the next men the life-changing, truly transformative weekend they had experienced.

"During the 48 hours of my NWTA, something happened to me that I will never forget. I was initiated into healthier, soulful, unabashed maleness. I gained pride and deep appreciation at being a man. I was invited to become more authentic, to throw aside the roles, conditioning, and expectations that had been placed on me by my family and culture and to discover my own truths. I discovered my life's Mission of Service and began the hard and abiding work of eliminating any blocks within me that prevented me from living my Mission more fully in the world. I became deeply connected with a circle of like-minded, openhearted, aware men who were committed to the same path I was. Most profound of all, I somehow was empowered to ground my thirty years of spiritual practice into the Earth, which felt like 250,000 volts of electricity passing through my body. I connected my spirituality to my soulfulness. I literally and figuratively became much more alive! I discovered and felt deeply submerged feelings of grief, fear, anger, and (surprisingly!) joy. I was given tools for expressing these feelings in safe, useful ways. The change in me was so immediate and so profound that I knew my life would never be the same. I found my passion! I felt aliveness and energy coursing through my body, heart, and soul that I had not previously imagined!

The man who came home from that weekend retreat was truly transformed in profound ways. I'll always remember my homecoming that Sunday afternoon. My wife was off visiting friends, so I sent the babysitter home, and I put my then three- and six-year-old daughters on my lap facing me and looked deeply into their eyes. They could feel my love flow like a vast river from my eyes to theirs. They soaked up my love like sponges, and they began to cry. Tears flowed down my face, as well, as I told my daughters how much I loved them, how precious they were to me, and how profoundly grateful I was to have them both in my life. They sat in my lap for close to an hour bathing in the love of their father. I was also able to express my love and appreciation more deeply, as well, to my wife and family and church and students.

How Discovering My Mission of Service Changed My Life

"I recognized something deeply moving: I was on fire with love and passion for my life. I became a much better father, husband, lover, teacher, and minister. It didn't happen overnight, but I was on a path that I committed to remain on for the remainder of my life. I continued to tear off that protective mask of perfection and to become more authentic and more present to the people in my life. And that was the beginning of reclaiming my passion—a process that continues to this day. My Mission of Service that I discovered that weekend is: I Create a Passionately Loving and Peaceful Planet by Fostering Safe, Sacred, Diverse Healing Circles. That Mission has served me deeply for over twenty years as I grew as a man and found my way to serving my family, my career, and this planet. (More on Mission later!)

"One brilliant innovation that MKP developed was the ongoing work and support following the NWTA, the

'Integration Group' or 'I-Group' for short. I joined twelve men from my NWTA weekend to form our I-Group. We were facilitated in integrating the teaching and tools of the weekend (by two of the men who staffed my weekend) for ten weeks. Then we were encouraged to continue on as a self-sustaining group. I am still in a powerful I-Group (with several men leaving and more joining) twenty-five years after I did my NWTA! These men are my closest friends, confidantes, and supporters. These men know me better than anyone else knows me. They reflect to me my 'shadows'—both dark and gold. They love me unconditionally. These men are there for me when I have losses and challenges. And I am there for them. They hold me accountable to my commitments, help me process my failures, and honor me for my accomplishments. Before my NWTA, I had virtually no male friends I trusted or cared for. After this training, I became surrounded by loving, strong, passionate men—hundreds of them. Being in this group has been truly transformative and completely life changing for me! It was a miracle!

"Soon after my initiatory weekend, I began to serve as a staff man for NWTAs as an attempt to give back some of the gifts that I had received. I also began to work toward becoming a Certified Leader in MKP by doing Leadership Training offered by the organization, continuing my own personal work, and pursuing other personal growth experiences outside MKP. I was certified as a Co-Leader of the NWTA in July 1992 and as a Full Leader in July 1993. Two years later, I completed the requirements to become a Leader

Trainer in MKP. My Mission of Service was coming ever more clearly into focus as I consciously found opportunities to 'foster safe, sacred, diverse healing circles' in my family, in my classroom, in my church, and in the workshops and trainings I led for MKP.

"I continue to lead NWTAs and Leadership Trainings for MKP all over the world to this day. It is a huge gift to be able to travel to many parts of the world working with alive, passionate men helping them to develop their own leadership and living their Missions more fully! Since 1990, I have staffed over 160 MKP trainings in most of the thirty-nine centers that MKP has across the United States and in seven other countries.

Some of My Healing Work

"During this time, I continued to 'go for' my own healing. I dove fiercely and fearlessly into my own personal growth, as I supported that of others. I continued to find and reclaim parts of myself that I had lost access to. I became more self-aware and much more willing to acknowledge my shortcomings and mistakes. By doing so, I shed the mountain of shame that held me back for so long. I cherished close and deep relationships with the men and women in my life who were on a similar path. I mentored many men and women and was mentored by many, as well. I learned how to give and receive support. I discovered my victim and my perpetrator, which had done so much damage unconsciously in my life. I made peace with most of my past and have moved toward living my Mission more fully in the world day by day. I became more of a human being—passionate, alive, engaged, authentic, and deeply connected with the world. I am deeply, deeply grateful for these changes in my life and the many people who supported me along the way. Teachers, mentors, friends, relatives, spiritual advisors, and confidantes—all have given me much in the way of teaching and modeling what an effective, powerful, and passionate life might look like. There are way too many to name here, but each one is remembered with huge gratitude, love, appreciation, and awe!

"I share this small part of my story to illustrate that I have myself struggled with living passionlessly and have found a path to reclaiming my passion, authenticity, and aliveness. I am still on that path and continue to 'do my own work' in many ways. I want to support you in doing the same! By doing so, I live my Mission while helping you to live yours. I committed a long time ago to 'living a big life'; to 'going for it'; to transparently and authentically use my struggles, my challenges, my failures, and my victories as an example of one way it can be done. I want to be an inspiration. I want to make a difference in this world. I want my children and grandchildren to have a better, safer, more sacred, more loving, and more alive world to live in. I suspect you do, too!"[9]

Now you know some pieces of my personal story and motivation. You have read some of my deep challenges that came out of my upbringing, about a few of my failures, and of my deep commitment to my own healing and growth. All of this life experience brought me to the point where I could integrate more fully the Seven Generations story into my life and healing process. I was ready to embrace the possibility that my own healing was inextricably linked to that of my family system—and perhaps the world. As I age and as I witness my daughters and granddaughters grow and express themselves more fully and more completely in the world, I have become more committed to doing my part in our Seven Generations story.

Since I wrote this personal history in 2011, there have been more changes in my life. I am divorced now from my second wife, all three of my daughters have graduated from college, and one is about to complete veterinary school soon. All three granddaughters are now in school and are growing and developing at a remarkable rate! I am so proud of them all! I have also moved from Wisconsin to San Diego, moving my business with me. More challenges to work on! Never a dull moment!

My familial history has lead me to change the focus and tenor of my healing work, albeit slightly. I now work with a mind toward healing not just myself, but my whole family system as well. I think and pray often about the seven generations that came before me, and the seven generations that shall follow. I am clear that my work is not just for me, but for my whole family line. I thrill to think that what I do today is influencing in a good way my grandparents, great-grandparents, and so on back 175 years, as well as my daughters, granddaughters, and so forth forward for 175 years. Isn't that an amazing thought? That thought energizes and potentizes my own healing work, and makes it very poignant for me to pursue.

In my first book, I wrote about the seven healing modalities (or Steps) I'm drawn to, so I won't go into detail here. However, I do think it worthwhile to outline these modalities so that my new readers can think about them and how you will initiate or continue your own healing in such a way to heal your own familial pain and history.

I've shared below a brief description of the seven steps I share and practice on a regular basis. For more detail, please see my first book.[9]

The Seven Healing Steps I Participate in as Part of My Daily Healing Regimen

1. Dedication to a Regular Daily Practice: I strongly advocate creating a daily practice that includes some form of meditation or reflection, breath work, and regular exercise. I firmly believe that starting my day with the rituals I have created for myself helps me to focus on gratefulness, forgiveness, my long-term goals, my Mission, and then plan my daily activities. In doing so, I reconnect with and acknowledge my Higher Power daily. I challenge myself to do this even when it is hard or gets in the way of daily activity. I feel energized, connected with my Higher Power and myself, grounded, and clearer when I do this regularly. I commit to my daily practice—the rewards are manifold.

2. Active Participation in Support Groups: I find consistent participation in several types of support groups incredibly valuable and important to my growth. I find deep connection, credible and compassionate feedback, and a sense of being valued and supported by attending circles of like-minded individuals. Of particular importance for me is being in groups of people who are as deeply invested in their own growth and emergence as I am, so that we develop long-term relationships that lead to clearer and deeper knowledge of each other's shadows, purpose, blind spots, value, and beauty.

3. Seeking Regular, Honest, Direct Feedback: I assiduously seek out and trust the feedback I get from people in my life on a regular basis. I willingly get others' feedback on my unconscious parts, as well as for help in decision making by asking for feedback from family, friends, and my support circles. This can be done through formal processes, like hot seats, feedback loops, or feedback circles, or informally through conversations and check-ins. Gathering feedback is a vulnerable yet courageous and powerful way to gain awareness of my unconsciousness, as well as helping chart my progress.

4. Continue to Work on Shadow Mining: I keep in the forefront the importance to my growth of fiercely seeking out my shadows: those parts of me I hide, repress, and deny; have lost awareness of; or have lost access to. I do this as courageously as possible through asking for feedback, by noticing on whom I project my darkness and my gold, and by being willing to become aware of my "intention versus my impact" on others. As I reclaim these vital parts of me lost through my early conditioning, abuse, and damaging messages, I notice greater access to my life energy, my capacities, my creativity, my joy, and my cultural competence.

5. Gaining Greater Multicultural Awareness: Another key part of my recovery is dedication to multicultural awareness or cultural competency. I cannot live in a world where inequality and harsh judgment of people different from me goes unchallenged. This work takes the personal level awareness and interpersonal level skills I have learned and broadens them to include the cultural realm, enlarging my influence and worldview, as well as putting my Mission work on a world stage. As I become aware of the places in my life where I have unearned privilege and the places where I am oppressed, I gain greater compassion for others and myself. I reclaim the parts of me that have been denigrated and oppressed by society. I also gain the capacity to understand and to become an ally to those in my life who face deep and damaging oppressions. I do this by reaching out to people who are different from me, reading and watching media on this topic, attending workshops, becoming socially active, engaging people in conversations about our "isms," and internally noticing when I dismiss or oppress people who are different from me.

6. Living in Radical Accountability and Integrity: I practice fierce and loving accountability in my life. I am dedicated to practicing an accountability process regularly, with the intent of holding myself to my agreements and goals. I do this through formal processes, listening to feedback from others, and noticing when my impacts seem to be different from my intentions. I commit to fulfilling my commitments! I also commit to living in integrity to the best of my ability: I say what I mean and mean what I say. My feelings, words, thoughts, and actions are congruent and transparent. I am willing to be vulnerable, even when I don't feel completely safe. I am willing to "turn myself in," when I become aware of dysfunctional behaviors or hurtful attitudes, to people I trust—and I listen carefully to their feedback.

7. Living Fully in My Golden Mission of Service: Perhaps most important of all, I choose to live my life as much as possible in alignment with my Golden Mission of Service. In doing so, I call on and align myself with my Higher Power. My purpose is clearly reflected in my Mission of Service. I regularly state my Mission and use it as a tool to evaluate my decisions and the direction of my life. I own my gold and honor my capacity to serve and change the world. I commit to putting my Mission out front even when it is difficult and inconvenient. (For a simple example, I sign all my emails with my name, contact information, and Mission statement.) I also keep my Shadow Mission in front of me by saying it regularly and noticing when I am acting out of my dark shadow. I regularly seek opportunities to serve and share my Mission with others. I seek opportunities to live my Mission by doing service work for my organizations, my community, and my family.

My friends, I can find no greater impetus for practicing these seven powerful steps than to effect healing for my family system, the planet, and myself. I truly believe that my healing is linked with that of my family heritage—for seven generations in both directions! I commit to continue all seven of my healing practices regularly, consciously, and with joy and the assurance that I am making a difference for my family … and the world. I lovingly invite you to explore which of these practices might work well for you and your own healing and growth—or to find your own practices that are different from mine. Won't you join me?

http://www.SevenGenerationsStory.com/

Chapter 2 Exercises

Exercise 6: Now's the time to capture your own personal stories. What are the seminal experiences that move you, hold you back, or motivate you? Share a few here and note the impact they have had on your life.

Exercise 7: (a). Which Healing Practices (or Steps) do you already incorporate into your life? How are they working to support your healing and growth? (b). Which of these practices scare or repel you? Why do you think that might be?

Exercise 8: Of those practices I recommend from my own life, which call to you? What practice might you add to your own healing regimen? How deeply will you commit to practicing whatever regimen you choose on a regular basis? In my experience, it works best to commit to a daily practice to both gain momentum and see maximum progress in your life!

Exercise 9: What is your Mission of Service? Don't worry about the form being perfect! Just think of a vision of the world that calls to you and an action you can/do take to make that vision a reality. Write it down and try it on for a while to see if it fits!

Chapter 3

More about How the Seven Generations Story Has Worked in My Life

"A particular pattern will continue to run in a family until the pattern is broken or resolved. Unfinished business from our ancestors can affect our lives and actually show up in our DNA. ... As we release unprocessed emotions, we are not only healing our lives but also healing the pain of untold generations as we give that gift to our descendants."
Dr. Ranae Johnson

"You can't heal the personality or relationships of one child without healing the whole family. The influence of the family tree is too strong. ... Most people have "psychic octopuses" that need to be cleared out of their personalities. Tentacles originating several generations back can still jerk you around like a puppet on a string. Because we are so entwined with our ancestors, we can't lift ourselves out of our harmful patterns without lifting our entire family tree out with us."
Denny Ray Johnson

The quotes above highlight the profound intergenerational aspects of healing that is so well described by the Seven Generation story. I am convinced of the validity of this thinking and research, even if it is at odds with my scientific training as a chemist! I have simply experienced too many incidents of healing happening in mysterious and amazing ways across family generations. I would like to share some more stories of how this has played out in my own life—both in terms of healing my own family heritage and myself—as well as healing work I've done with many other people who have attended workshops and talks I have had the privilege of leading over many years.

For example, I have lead over 200 initiatory, multicultural, and leadership trainings for the ManKind Project[TM] (MKP)[9] all over the world in the past twenty-five years. It has been a great privilege and joy to lead the fine trainings this international not-for-profit offers. (In fact, I am one of just two men across the planet who are certified to lead every training MKP has to offer—the other being my very good friend, Henry Thurman.) I have lead about 170 New Warrior Training Adventures (NWTA), which is MKP's initiation training for men. It is the "gateway" training that all men are required to attend first to become initiated into a healthier maleness, discover their Missions of Service, and so much more. The men can then choose to get into an "Integration Group" (I-Group), which is an ongoing group of men who typically went through the NWTA together and meet weekly or bi-weekly. Men are then eligible to do some of the other six trainings MKP has to offer. These include the five leadership trainings the organization offers (Staff Trainings 1 & 2 and Leadership Trainings 1, 2, & 3), as well as a multicultural awareness training called "Isms and Issues: An Introduction to Multicultural Awareness" that is required for all men going into leadership in the organization. I've lead about fifty leadership trainings for MKP, as well as about forty "Isms & Issues" over the years.

In addition, I've led dozens of trainings for other organizations, including my own company. Topics include Meditation and Breath Work workshops, Mission Workshops, Multicultural Awareness Trainings, Money Shadow Workshops, Authentic Appreciation Workshops, Emotional Intelligence Seminars, Learning Love Workshops, working inside prisons, and many others.

What Is Transformation?

Why do I mention this? Because each of these trainings contains cathartic, transformational processes that help men and women move from an old to a new way of being. I've witnessed tremendous, seemingly magical and deeply moving healing occur for participants in these trainings—many, many times! In my experience, to accomplish this requires authentic and deep emotional expression accompanied by truthful re-scripting or reinterpretation of the meaning of life events and traumas we all experience. The ancestral aspect of these healings is not always obvious. However, for many of the processes I've witnessed and led, there often is a direct link between the healing of a participant and the generational wounds of their family.

Through all of this leading over so many years, and along with my own deep dive into my personal work, I have become a master at facilitating transformational processes with men and women seeking lasting change in their lives! I say this humbly, but truthfully. I have learned how to create safe, sacred, diverse containers that strongly, yet gently invite people into being authentic and vulnerable. I have facilitated and witnessed so many profound healings that I know I can act as a conduit to some Higher Power that resides both within and outside myself. I know these transformations are not happening due to me! Somehow, the right words are said, the correct process is chosen for the participant, and real healing happens. It is an amazing joy and a deep privilege to be part of such healing events!

A Healing Process in Prison

Randy, a forty-five-year-old convicted felon was a participant in a training I helped lead in a federal prison in Massachusetts in 2002. In the first process of our weekend-long training, Randy chose me to be his "dog," or mentor/support man for the weekend. When it came time to choose his dog, he immediately walked across the prison compound and stood in front of me. He later said, "I knew immediately that you were my 'dog.' I could see in your eyes that you were a safe man to work with. And I need safety, since I am a gay man—and if that got out into the general population of this prison, I would likely be a dead man within days!" I was both moved and a bit puzzled as to why Randy was disclosing this sensitive information to me, after knowing me for less than a minute! He explained, "What I need to do this weekend is very important work for my own well-being, as well as for [my] family. I want to make full use of you and this amazing opportunity, and to do so, I am ready to be authentic and completely open!" Wow!

As the weekend proceeded, I learned more of Randy's sad story. He had been in a committed relationship with Josh for fifteen years. Randy had been a cocaine addict before he met Josh, but he had gotten clean and sober and had practiced the twelve steps for over eighteen years. Randy was a tile installer and made a decent living doing tile work. Josh and he were very much in love, and they were saving for a new home. Life seemed good for them both.

I then learned that a year before he went to prison, Randy had a relapse. Josh was unaware of the relapse, and Randy kept it secret since Josh committed to leaving Randy if he started using coke again. As Randy slipped deeper into his addiction, he began to take money from their house fund to buy drugs. This continued until Randy had spent all their savings.

Randy looked at me carefully before continuing, gauging my reaction to his story. When he seemed satisfied that I was listening without negative judgment, he continued, "I was terrified that Josh would find out and leave me. I knew it would devastate him, yet I could not seem to stop! When the last of our savings was used up, I panicked and decided to do the only thing I could think of to replenish our nest egg—rob a bank!" I listened attentively to Randy as he shared this painful story. "The first bank robbery went well. I escaped with $6,000, but that was not nearly enough to bring our account back to its previous level. So I robbed another bank, and another—six times successfully! It was that seventh bank robbery where I got caught, arrested, and jailed."

I took a deep breath but continued to look directly into Randy's eyes as he moved on with his story. "I was completely emotionally devastated. I had failed at my sobriety, lost our nest egg, committed seven felonies, and gotten caught! I didn't know what to do, so I called Josh from jail and told him that I had been arrested for some unpaid parking tickets. I was that afraid of telling Josh the truth!"

Randy continued, "Eventually, I was tried, convicted, and sent to prison for twelve years. Josh, despite his pain at being betrayed so deeply, came to the trial and supported me throughout. However, on the day of my verdict and sentence, he apparently couldn't take anymore, and he went home and hung himself! My partner of fifteen years had committed suicide ... and I knew it was my fault. Worse yet, I was imprisoned and was not allowed to go to Josh's funeral and grieve his death. That happened two years ago, and I have felt really depressed and lifeless—even more so than one in prison should be."

As Randy shared this last piece of his story, tears welled up in my eyes in compassion for my new friend. I could not fully understand how Randy could have sunk so low nor how he survived such trauma, yet my empathy for him grew! I was not at all surprised he was depressed and feeling like life was no longer worth living. I also felt deep respect for this man who was sharing this painful story with a stranger so very freely. I was frankly amazed at Randy's openness in the face of his very daunting experiences. And, I must also admit, I was more than a little puzzled at how a seemingly stable and productive man could fall so far so quickly!

I took a deep breath and asked Randy, "So what are you looking for from this weekend?" He replied (as I suspected) that he thought he needed to grieve Josh's death. Soon after our exchange, we were moved into a group room where our transformational work would take place on a "magic carpet." Randy was the first man up, and he asked me to facilitate his work as ten other staff men and inside men looked on and supported him. I turned to him and asked him to list the impacts (consequences) of his actions on himself and on his partner. His list was long and painful to recite! By the time he completed his list, he was deeply in tears.

Then I asked him to pick a man to stand in for his dead

partner, Josh. I placed that man flat on his back on the carpet and covered him with a blanket. I then turned to Randy and asked him if he (Randy) was now fully alive? He hesitated then replied, "Not really. I often feel dead. In fact, it feels like a large part of me is in the grave with Josh."

I asked Randy to lie down next to Josh's still figure, and I covered him up with the blanket. I quietly left him there for a few moments then asked, "How does this feel, Randy?"

He responded, "This feels just like my life! It also feels pretty good to be dead and not feeling anything!" This last part seemed to be a revelation to Randy, so I asked him to speak about the parts of him that were "dead and in the grave," and he said, "My heart and soul are dead. So are my spontaneity, my sense of passion, my zest for living, and my compassion for others—and for myself."

After listening to Randy's list, I said, "Those are some very important parts of you that are dead!"

"Yes," he replied, "I hadn't fully realized this was true until you asked."

I continued, "A big piece of you is in the grave with Josh, isn't it?" He agreed by nodding. I continued, "This often happens when we feel responsible for another's death, and we haven't grieved the loss well. Randy, do you want to be fully alive? Do you want access to your aliveness, your passion, and all the other things you listed as lost?" At this point, Randy's tears started flowing again as he nodded forcefully. Then I had him move out from under the cover and kneel next to the still-covered form representing his partner, Josh. I told Randy that we could magically bring Josh back to life for a few minutes just so that Randy could say what he wanted to say to him and grieve his passing fully.

I had Randy close his eyes, then I pulled the blanket down just far enough to reveal "Josh's" face. I whispered to the man playing Josh to open his eyes and look at Randy. I instructed Randy to look at Josh when he was ready and to say whatever he felt he needed to say to bring closure to his relationship with Josh. Randy opened his eyes and looked into Josh's eyes intently for a few moments. As tears welled up in his eyes, he then said to Josh, "I'm so very sorry, Josh! I love you so much, but I let my addiction get the best of me, and I know I hurt you deeply. It was not my intention, but I feel so sad that I hurt the very person I loved the most! Will you forgive me? Please?" I asked Randy if there was anything else he was withholding from Josh. "Yes! I am angry at you, Josh, for choosing the coward's way out. I am so angry and hurt that you killed yourself!" Randy began to sob uncontrollably at this point. I had the man playing Josh hold out his hands slowly toward Randy as if he wanted a hug. At this point, Randy fell into Josh's embrace and placed his head on Josh's chest. His sobbing deepened. Josh hugged Randy to his heart, but he said nothing as Randy grieved his lost partner deeply. After several minutes of this, Randy pulled back a bit so that he could see Josh's eyes. "Do you forgive me, Josh?" Josh's representative nodded slowly and lovingly. "Do you still love me?" Josh nodded again.

I then stated, "Perhaps Josh needs your forgiveness, too?"

Randy considered this thought for a moment, then tuned to Josh and said, "I also forgive you for killing yourself! I don't understand fully, and I am still deeply sad, but I forgive you, my love."

At this, Randy lightened considerably. His sobbing subsided. I said to Randy, "Now comes the hard part. You need to let Josh go, knowing that his suicide was his choice completely. Then I invite you to metaphorically pull yourself out of this grave and make a clear choice to live your life fully and passionately in Josh's honor and to fulfill your own destiny and life's purpose. Can you do that? Can you see that Josh really wants you to do that?"

Randy considered my invitation for a very short time then turned to Josh's figure and said, "Josh, again, I love you and forgive you for leaving. That was your choice, and, while I love you, I must let go of my guilt and shame. I must pull myself out of this grave and choose to live fully. I choose to reclaim the parts of me I let die in your honor: I reclaim my heart and my soul. I also reclaim my spontaneity, my sense of passion, my zest for living, and my compassion for others. I must reclaim these parts of me to live fully, Josh." At this point, Randy's energy shifted again. As he reclaimed each lost part of himself, he straightened up a bit more, and his energy soared. Finally, he seemed complete with Josh. He said a final goodbye to his partner and lover and covered him up again with the blanket.

I asked Randy to stand up and to take the posture of a fully alive man in the center of the circle. He did so and then spontaneously raised his hands into the air and yelled, "I am alive! I choose to be fully alive!" He turned around, repeating this phrase several times as he made eye contact with all the men supporting him around the carpet. His eyes radiated light and life as Randy's energy once again shifted dramatically at this point. He was smiling broadly as he claimed his aliveness in front of the circle of men who were composed of some staff as well as other inmates ("inside men"). He appeared very energized, fully alive, and surprisingly joyful! The men in the circle then cheered happily for Randy. At this point, Randy's process seemed complete. He had completed unfinished business with his partner, said what he needed to say to him, grieved Josh's passing, and reclaimed his own aliveness!

The transformation was palpable and powerful. During the course of his process, Randy's posture changed from a head-down position, shoulders slumped, and making virtually no eye contact with men, to head up, shoulders back, and looking every man directly in the eyes. The change in his face was even more stunning as he shifted from deep sadness with lifeless eyes, to open, smiling, totally alive, and amazingly joyful! He stayed that way during the entire weekend and, I'm told, for long after that training experience.

I was truly grateful to have played a part in Randy's healing as well as to have witnessed his truly transformational work. I also had no doubt that his partner's spirit, wherever it was, felt this release and was healed in part as well! I am smiling as I recall this process and this amazing day. Randy's was just one of many healing processes I witnessed and supported during the course of that weekend for these incarcerated men whom society had branded as unworthy, unredeemable, and of no value. My attitude about men in prison changed much that day. I saw how much like me these men were, and how easily I could have ended up just like them. It was very moving to assist these men in their healing—especially since many of them would never again set foot outside that prison. This was a truly amazing gift!

A Healing Process with One of My Daughters

There are prisons inside each of us that are just as restricting as the one Randy was in. Without doubt, the most painful episode of my life is the estrangement from my oldest daughter, Erica. With all the healing work I have done in the world for others and with all my own healing work over thirty years, I have not been able to heal my relationship with my daughter, very sadly. This estrangement began in her early teens and continues through today as she enters her thirties. To add to the pain of this separation, she has a ten-year-old daughter, Skye, whom I love dearly, whom I have not seen for four years. My granddaughter is bright and beautiful and very smart (like her mother!), but I do not get to interact with her at all. Even so, I feel strongly that I have had some very positive influence on both my daughter and granddaughter—further evidence supporting the validity of the Seven Generations story!

For example, when Erica was sixteen years old, she decided to join in on a summer backpacking/science course I taught for thirty years. For this class, I took twelve high school–aged boys and girls on a ten-day, 100-mile backpacking trip in the Kettle-Moraine State Park in Wisconsin where we did science activities (I taught chemistry for 35 years!), as well as leadership building and healing processes that I added to the curriculum. This trip was the only one I did that had just young women attending. I decided to let Erica have her own experience and placed her in a team of three other girls, all of whom I knew from chemistry classes I taught at my high school.

During this trip, I introduced some of the healing modalities I had been learning and practicing in my life and in my healing circles. After getting up at the crack of dawn, we hiked our ten miles for the day early, before it got too hot, then we did our science activities, and then, after dinner and around the campfire, I shared with these students some of my "other work." This was entirely voluntary, of course, but virtually all the students loved the healing and leadership-building work I brought to the campfire and embraced it fully and enthusiastically. On the first night, I taught these students the concept of confidentiality and how to "check in." They were invited to state their name and how they were feeling. This was also the place to bring any conflicts that were bothering class members so that we could problem solve any difficulties together, so that the class flowed more smoothly and consciously.

On the second night, I did a visualization with these kids so that they could choose an animal spirit to support them during the class and afterwards. I brought along my "Animal Speaks"[10] and the "Medicine Cards and Book"[11] so that students could look up the totem animal they chose to see how well it "fit" them. Rarely did a student fail to see how their totem animal's characteristics described their personalities and life challenges, as well as how it fit where they were in their lives!

I'd like to interject a quick story here about Mike, a fifteen-year-old young man who attended a different trip, and his experience in this process. Mike was the son of a school board member and was a member of a very conservative Christian church in town. So I was not at all surprised at Mike's resistance to the Animal Names process, which smacked of shamanism to him. Though suspicious and a bit reluctant, he nevertheless participated in the process, and his animal name became owl. Later, when all the students had found their animal names, I shared with them that they could read about their animals in the two books I brought for them. I also suggested that they should stay alert to any messages they might receive from their totem animals through either direct contact during our trip or in their dreams. Mike expressed his skepticism, and I simply allowed him to be in this place of not understanding, as that was clearly where he needed to be. I did notice, however, that Mike listened attentively to every other classmate as they excitedly shared their animal totems and what they had learned about that connection.

The next morning we were up as usual at 6:00 a.m. and on the trails by 7:00 a.m. We hadn't hiked 100 yards when a feather floated down from the tree canopy and landed at Mike's feet. The hiking line stopped as Mike picked up the feather and handed it to me. "Mr. Broniec," he said, "what kind of feather is this?" I took one look at it, and the hair on the back of my neck stood up.

I replied, "Well, Mike, that is an owl feather. Both great horned and bard owls live in these woods, but I'm quite certain that this is a great horned owl feather!" That's all I said, but the students in the class all expressed surprise at this gift landing at Mike's feet. From that point forth on the trip, Mike paid respectful and enthusiastic attention to my every word! I am still amazed as I remember this miraculous story that happened some fifteen years ago!

Now back to Erica's story. By the third night, students were quite strongly bonded and connected, and we moved on to help them find their Golden Missions of Service. This is a powerful and quite sacred process that I had taught for many years in men's and couple's workshops I facilitated—and a process my students just loved. With the help of a few visualizations I led, and the support of their team members, each student crafted a wonderful Golden Mission of Service that stated their reasons for being on the planet. It was a moving process and a real gift for these young people to discover their Missions of Service at such a young age. As I remember it, Erica's Golden Mission was: "I create a loving planet by being a loving and helpful person to all." This was a revealing and powerful statement for a young woman who was acting out so much of the time at home and in school! Even so, I was delighted that Erica was participating fully in all the activities of the trip—especially those around the campfire! And I was especially thankful that she had found such a wonderful Mission of Service! I sensed her ancestors at work within her.

One of Erica's teammates was Nicole, a wonderful and inspiring young woman who had almost died of leukemia the year before. Nicole had spent her junior year in high school healing from her leukemia. She was near death at one point, but was saved by a bone-marrow transplant. Nicole was healthy enough to complete her senior year of high school the next year. Near the end of that year, she approached me about joining my annual summer ten-day backpacking/science trip. She told me she wanted to attend, even though she was officially graduated from high school and would get no credit, to prove to herself that she had fully recovered by facing the challenges of backpacking 100 miles over ten days. I was really delighted to have Nicole join us and immediately put Erica in her group so that they could get to know each other.

I had become accustomed to the enthusiasm with which these young people would approach the process of creating their Mission statements. During this evening process, we came to the point where the students combined their vision with their actions to create their Golden Missions of Service for the first time. At that moment, Nicole burst into tears and began to sob uncontrollably for a good ten minutes. She leaned on the shoulder of a fellow hiker as she sobbed. The circle bore silent witness to Nicole's freely flowing tears.

When she was done, I asked her if she wished to share what was going on for her. She nodded her head. After a few moments of quiet reflection, she said, "When God spared my life last year, I knew at a deep level that I had been saved for a reason—that I had some important purpose for being on this planet, but I didn't know what it was until this very moment." Nicole paused thoughtfully for a moment and then continued, "My Golden Mission of Service is to Create a Healthy Planet by Healing Myself, the Sick, and the Needy." Then she began to cry again, though this time not alone, as we all joined her in deeply joyful tears, celebrating that this wonderful young woman was alive and well and with us at this moment in time, activated by such a powerful Mission. This was one of many incredibly sacred moments I had the privilege of participating in or witnessing during this class over the years—and certainly one of my most treasured highlights!

As an aside, Nicole kept in touch with me as she entered college at Marquette University in Milwaukee, Wisconsin. She graduated and went on to medical school. A few years later, I got a note from Nicole that she had graduated from medical school and was starting her career as a medical doctor! She said, "Little did I know that my health crisis as a teenager would lead me to a dream career as a doctor healing others' illnesses! Thanks, Mr. B, for helping me find my Golden Mission that guided me to my life's career!" Amen to that, Nicole! After this process was complete, each student then checked in with his/her name, animal name, and Golden Mission, twice a day for the remainder of the trip.

Now, back again to Erica's story. We always did a ritual on the last night of this backpack trip where each student checked out by stating whatever it was they wanted to say about what they were taking away from their ten-day experience. They were also encouraged to speak to each classmate to share the impact that person had on them. There was rarely a dry eye around that last campfire as students poured out their gratitude and amazement about all the things that had transpired during our trip. The loving and deep connections were palpable as these precious kids spoke. Most of the students included me in their comments, which were universally thankful and very appreciative for the safe, inviting container I helped create, as well as for the open and accepting energy I emanated. It always felt great to hear these young people share how impactful the trip was for them—especially my contributions!

Erica was the last person to check out. She was thoughtful, emotional, and very sincere as she spoke to each participant. Then, much to my surprise, my daughter, who had been so distant and judgmental about her father, turned to me and spoke directly to me as she looked into my eyes across the campfire. "Dad, I am so proud of you for creating this trip and for helping us all get so close. You are amazing at creating a safe and sacred space that helps us all feel safe. I am so glad I came on this trip! You also blessed us with your deep knowledge of science along with the beautiful process/healing work we did each night. But what I want to say to you most is I love you very much. I know I haven't said that recently, but it's true." Needless to say, my friends, I was deeply moved by Erica's words. I honestly did not know that she still felt this way about me, even though we had been very close when she was younger.

So once again, I saw the incredible power of the Seven Generations story! I was watching my precious, but troubled daughter heal before my eyes as she proclaimed her love for me, the man with whom she was often at serious odds. From that time forth, I knew deep within that Erica would be fine and that our love connection was present within us both, even if she was not able to express it to me directly. I also knew, later on when she had her own daughter, that that grandchild would be raised in a loving and supportive manner. I didn't have to worry about my granddaughter! I am forever grateful for that reminder that Erica and I are connected and mutually loving to this day, whether we speak or not.

The Multi-Generational Healing of One Family

On one of the New Warrior Adventure Trainings I led for the ManKind Project a few years ago, there was a twenty-four-year-old man (Tom) and his fifty-two-year-old father (Steve) staffing together. They had invited their seventy-five-year-old father and grandfather (Mike) to attend the training as an initiate, and they were so delighted and, frankly, a bit challenged to staff his weekend. When it came time for Mike to do his transformational carpet work, Tom and Steve were sequestered out of sight (as was often the convention) so that their presence did not inhibit Mike's healing work. I was deeply impressed by Mike's willingness to "go for" his healing. This was not an easy thing to do for a man raised in the era he was raised in!

Mike dove into some deeply hidden pain he had carried all his life about being excluded and harshly judged as a child due to his having a speech impediment. This affliction, coupled with his being a Polish immigrant with a thick accent, caused Mike to feel different, unlovable, and defective. Mike's parents also suffered much the same wounds, exacerbated by living through the Great Depression and World Wars I and II. This dynamic had profound effects on his life. Mike, like so many other men raised in our culture, felt isolated and unloved and had a very hard time expressing his feelings—especially the tender feelings of love and care and joy that he had been denied as a child. He felt bad that he had passed these same wounds on to his son and grandson. He knew at a heart level that he needed to reclaim his sweet, innocent, loving self, but there were loud voices of hatred and very hurtful ostracizing actions from his childhood that played over and over in his head like a CD stuck on replay. (I am aware of such voices in my head, too! How about you?) Mike somehow knew his work was to silence these messages, symbolized by the voices of his cruel classmates in the elementary schoolyard. We had Mike choose a few men to represent those kids. He placed them in the center of the carpet, blocking him from getting to an "ideal dad" that he had chosen earlier, who could love him unconditionally.

Mike's work was to cast those voices out so intently and with such deep emotion that they would never impede him again. He chose to do this by using his voice and eyes to force the men playing the taunting students off the carpet (and out of his life!). These students were instructed not to move until they felt such a deep resolve and crescendo in Mike's voice and demeanor that they knew unmistakably that transformation was occurring. Mike called up all his power, his anger, his ancestral support, and his self-love to do this work. It was a true joy to watch this older man access these parts of himself—for the first time in over sixty years! Mike looked directly at the three "classmates" standing between him and the loving father he so desperately needed. They had been given lines by Mike to say earlier like "You're stupid and a retard," and "I don't like you. You don't deserve friends. Just leave."

After several moments of shouting, "Shut up! I am a good man who deserves love!" at them, he reached a point where he knew he'd "never again" hear these voices. This was a point of deep knowing within Mike that these negative messages about him were false and he could choose to replace them with messages of love and support and inclusion. Magically, the voices ceased to exist! Transformation had occurred.

At that moment, the three taunting classmates silently left the carpet, leaving nothing between Mike and his "ideal dad." Mike walked quickly across the carpet to the smiling, inviting man playing his loving dad and fell into his arms. He began to sob deeply as he took in the messages he had wanted to hear all his life. "You are my precious son, Mike. I love you unconditionally, my son. I am proud of you and all you've accomplished in your life. You are wonderful and lovable just the way you are! I love you!" Mike soaked in these words of affirmation. It was clear that they were going deeply into his soul, creating a new "CD" of positive, loving, and generative words that were Mike's real truth! This was a sacred moment, and all the men around Mike's carpet simply held space for him as he fully embraced his new way of being.

When Mike had filled himself up with his ideal father's love and support, he then turned to the men in the circle and said powerfully and so sincerely, "I am a loved and loving man and I belong!" three times. The circle responded with loud cheering as each witness affirmed Mike in the circle with deep love and total acceptance.

But I knew intuitively that Mike's process was not complete yet, for Mike's wound had been passed down from his parents and grandparents through him to his son and grandson, who had come to their own weekends to heal almost identical messages that they had carried. So I asked Mike to close his eyes and think of some men with whom he might want to share his newfound love. As Mike contemplated that question silently, I quickly whisked both Tom and Steve onto the carpet to stand behind Mike. When Mike opened his eyes, he stated, with tears in his eyes, "Yes, I really want to share this incredible love and acceptance with my son and grandson! They deserve this healing too!"

"Well, Mike," I suggested, "I invite you to turn around." As he did so, he saw his son and grandson standing in front of him with big smiles on their faces and their arms wide open, beckoning to their father and grandfather. Mike literally ran to his offspring and fell into their arms for a deep embrace that had been waiting many years to happen. The joy and healing that occurred that day for the three generations of Mike's family was deeply moving to witness. Most men in the supporting circle had tears in their eyes, and they spontaneously moved in to join a massive group hug in the center of the carpet, celebrating Mike's, Tom's, and Steve's mutual healing! And I knew, once again, that all the men present and I were taking part in this incredible inter-generational healing. It was flowing right into our own hearts, for we all carried similar wounds and could rejoice that Mike's family's healing mirrored our own! This was another one of those "Hallmark moments" where I felt so grateful to be alive and doing this work! And I had a deep sense that my ancestors, as well as those of all the men on that weekend, were smiling down on us with great pride, deep love, and tremendous joy.

Some Healing Work with My Mother

In the Introduction to this book, I shared a moving and poignant story about my father's healing and how I was able to support him to share a very painful story of his childhood. I am so grateful to have had the experience of sharing this time and experience with my father and of stepping into greater healing of my relationship with him. I also am grateful for having had some powerful healing with my mother that I believe also supports the Seven Generations story. My mother passed on at the age of eighty-five in June 2014, just a few months before I wrote this section. I miss her very much! Even so, my mother was mentally ill for much of her life. She was never diagnosed officially, but most of her children believe she was suffering from schizophrenia. The many unusual manifestations of her illness made it difficult for us to be in a relationship with her, even though she loved all six of her children dearly and often expressed that! Just as an example, my mom had not seen a doctor for forty-four years, due to her belief that God (whom she talked to out loud and often!) would heal her, so she didn't need doctors. Sadly, she died of an abdominal infection that could have been easily treated with antibiotics if she had availed herself of traditional medical care before it was too late!

In the mid-1990s, soon after I began my healing journey, my mother began to tell my siblings individually when they visited her that she knew she had "hurt Rick by her parenting in ways she was ashamed of" and needed to make amends to me. Over a period of several months, she repeatedly spoke to my siblings about her feelings, but did not approach me at all to talk about her feelings. I suspect she was afraid of my reaction and, perhaps, feared I would react angrily.

After several of my siblings told me of Mom's curious comments, I decided to approach her directly to see if she wanted to spend some time with me alone so that she could unburden herself of whatever she wanted to share with me. She seemed very relieved when I called her and asked for some one-on-one time. We set up a meeting, and I drove the three and half hours to my mother and father's home in central Wisconsin. To my surprise, she had her hair done up and was dressed as if she were going out on New Year's Eve! She had shooed my father out of the house for a few hours so that we could meet alone. Apparently, this meeting was very important to her!

I began our conversation by asking Mom what it was she wanted to say to me about my upbringing. She immediately broke down in tears and began to confess what she thought were her transgressions against me, her eldest child. I simply let her speak for about an hour, listening carefully to the incidents and actions she believed had hurt me most during my upbringing. She was tearful and very humble as she confessed to me. When she was complete, I asked her, ""Mom, what do you want from me?""

She replied, "I'd like your forgiveness, Ricky. Please forgive me for my ignorance, my mistakes, and for learning how to parent at your expense." Her crying turned to sobs then.

Now it was my turn to cry! I turned to my mother and lovingly told her my truth. "Mom, I forgive you completely for any hurt you think you caused me. I know beyond a shadow of a doubt, Mom, that you loved me. You told me—and all your children—that often. I also believe that you did the best you could do with the understanding and tools at your disposal! So I forgive you and love you very much. In addition, I am grateful to you for raising me. It was not easy raising six kids, especially when you and Dad were separated so much of the time!"

Then I continued, "Mom, I think it would be useful for you to know that the incidents that you shared weren't the ones that hurt me the most." I then shared with her the things she had done (and, in some cases, had continued to do) that I believe had caused me pain. I gently shared my experiences with her and asked her to change a few behaviors toward me—and her other children and grandchildren. (For example, she had a hard time allowing her children to be adults. She constantly talked to me and about me as if I were still that ten-year-old little helper she loved and needed so much! I was forty years old, an award-winning teacher, married, and a father two times over, and she still insisted on calling me by my childhood nickname, "Ricky," despite my many protestations to stop over the years!) She was surprised, but listened carefully and then agreed to work at changing some of her behaviors. At this, my mom stopped crying and reached out to hug me closely to her. She expressed her thanks profoundly to me, and our conversation seemed to be complete! I'll never forget the look of appreciation on her face as we embraced one more time before I started home. I felt really good about this conversation with my mom. I suspect our ancestors were also quite pleased!

I noticed often during the next few months that my mom was truly trying to change her behaviors. I saw her slowly transform, and that change followed her for the remainder of her life. (She called me "Rick" from that day on!) Our relationship matured from that day forth. She began treating me as an equal adult and was much more respectful toward my family and me as a result of our conversation!

Now fast-forward twenty years to 2014. Just before she passed, I had a couple days with my mom in her hospice care facility in central Wisconsin. She was weak, but delighted to see me. I held her hand, sang hymns to her, read her favorite books, looked at family picture albums with her, and reminisced about our family. And I prayed with her. She laughed and cried and told stories as she faded in and out of consciousness. She asked me if I thought God loved her! I told her, "Of course he does, Mom. And, it's okay to let go and go home. It's time!" It was a precious and memorable few days together.

When it was time for me to go and catch my plane back to California, she awakened just long enough for me to tell her I loved her. She squeezed my hand and gave me a kiss and hug. Her last words to me were, "I love you, son!" There was little else I needed to hear from my mother, as we had no unfinished business. I left with great peace in my heart and gratitude for the healing we were able to do together so many years ago—and since! My beautiful mother passed on just three days later.

I have had numerous opportunities to test the Seven Generations story in my life, with people I've had the privilege of working with in so many capacities and with my own family. I am very grateful for the resolution and growth I have experienced that has filtered down to generations of my family—and many others—in both directions!

http://www.SevenGenerationsStory.com/

Chapter 3 Exercises

Exercise 10: Journal in the space below some of your own healing journeys. How has your life been impacted by your ancestors' wounds or healing?

Exercise 11: Detail below how parts of you might be "dead" or "in prison." What needs to come alive for you to live the life you were meant to live?

Exercise 12: What messages do you carry that block you from living fully or living your Mission of Service completely on this planet? What can you do to change these messages?

Chapter 4

Some Powerful Modes of Healing That Can Affect You and Seven Generations of Your Family

"We have the power to change the stories written in our genes and therefore the power to change our lives. An emotional history has been handed down to us through our family lineage. We can change our code. It is not set in stone. Revolutionary research is showing that our emotions impact us from the most basic level of our DNA, a finding that has far reaching ramifications."
Margaret Ruby, "The DNA of Healing"

"Hurt People hurt people. This is how pain patterns get passed on, generation after generation, after generation. Break the chain today. Meet anger with sympathy, contempt with compassion, cruelty with kindness. Greet grimaces with smiles. Forgive and forget about finding fault. Love is the weapon of the future."
Yehuda Berg

You've read this far, my friends, so I assume you have some investment in the Seven Generations story. Perhaps you believe the premise that what you do to heal yourself will also heal generations of your family in both directions. You may even have clear evidence of this truth from your own life experience. The beauty and poignancy of this concept moves you and calls to you, I hope. Maybe you can even see the future of your family system changing positively through your own efforts to heal your trans-generational wounds and stories. If so, good for you!

So, the next obvious question is: "What are some modes of healing that you might use to heal yourself and seven generations of your family—both past and future? What are the tools and processes you recommend, Rick, to help me, and my family along this amazing process? How do I start? How do I get support? And how do I know that progress is occurring? How do I free myself—and my family—from the 'psychic octopuses' that Denny Rae Johnson refers to in his quote above? How do I heal the 'emotional history' of my family and actually change the DNA code of our lineage, as described by Margaret Ruby?"

These are all very excellent questions. I have them myself! I have explored quite a few healing modalities over the years, and there are several I highly recommend—processes that are effective, safe, and deep enough to aid my own healing and put the Seven Generations story to work healing my family's intergenerational pain, suffering, and the persistent stories we all seem to carry. I believe along the way I've "broken the chains" of much of my family's emotional story, and I've learned to forgive and forget the old stuff that had previously held me back, as Yehuda Berg shared above. His statement, "Hurt

People Hurt People," is profound. The hopeful analog to Berg's assertion is, in my words, "Healed People Heal People."

The list I will share is not meant to be exhaustive in any way. However, out of my own sense of integrity, I will suggest and recommend only healing processes that I have experienced personally myself. Perhaps you have tried other modes that work for you; if so, "good on you," as my Australian friends say! Please share these with me so that I can try them out and add them to my list. Some of my recommendations were briefly mentioned in Chapter 2. I want to expand on those and add a couple more I have felt drawn to. Here goes!

A. Dedication to a Regular Daily Practice

Long ago, I committed to starting my day with a regular practice that grounds me, reminds me why I am alive, and focuses my day and my energy. That practice is critical to my healing and to maintaining my equanimity in this chaotic world. My own practice consists of meditation and breath work, along with repeating my Missions of Service to myself (more on Missions below). This practice not only calms and grounds me, but it allows me to touch my gratitude at being alive; at having been given this life, this body, this mind, and this soul to learn and grow and serve. I have so much to be grateful for—a healthy body; a clear, bright, intelligent mind; and an intuitive, empathetic, and compassionate soul. I have prosperity and health, love and friendship, a good education, and important work to do in this world. I am blessed beyond measure! Plugging into that gratitude every day elevates my spirits and my consciousness and reminds me that there is something far greater than myself at work here.

I don't believe the type of meditation you practice is critical; just having a process where you slow your breath and your mind and calm your body is what's important, in my experience. So try out Transcendental Meditation, Yogic meditation, Christian prayer, Buddhist sits, or any other practice that calls to you. Since I was seven years old, I have been meditating—long before it was accepted or cool. As I stated earlier in Chapter 2, my family joined a Self-Realization Fellowship (SRF) church in 1959. In 1968, I was initiated as a Kriya Yogi (Kriyaban) when I became old enough. I am no longer officially a part of the SRF organization (even though I now live just a few miles from their world headquarters in Encinitas, California, and often go to the beautiful meditation gardens there on the shores of the Pacific Ocean to meditate), but I thankfully and avidly practice Kriya meditation almost every day. That combination of quiet sitting and Kriya breath really serves to get me in a frame of mind to focus my day in a positive manner, while oxygenating and calming my mind. I also add some Rebirthing breath to my practice (more on that process below).

During the course of the day, when things get stressful or chaotic, I almost automatically return to my calming breathing and meditative state. I find that when life gets most chaotic and scary is when my meditation practice serves me the best. Try it, my friends. It works!

B. Active Participation in Support Groups

Whether you are part of a twelve-step program, a therapy group, or a men's or women's circle, I believe you will find that consistent participation in support groups will be incredibly valuable and important to your growth and well-being. I find deep connection, credible and compassionate feedback, and a sense of being valued and supported by other open-minded people whenever I attend circles of like-minded individuals. Of particular importance for me is being in groups of people who are as deeply invested in their own growth and emergence as I am, so that we develop long-term relationships that lead to clearer and deeper knowledge of each other's shadows, purpose, Missions, blind spots, value, and beauty.

I have gotten much from twelve-step groups (particularly Al-Anon), but I have gained the most from my participation in my MKP Integration Group (I-Group, for short). I was in the same I-Group for almost twenty-five years in Milwaukee, Wisconsin. My best friends— the men I know best and who know me very, very well, love me unconditionally, and call me on my destructive and unhealthy shadow behaviors—were my I-Group brothers. They also supported me through the deaths of my father and my mother, my divorces, illnesses, and so much more. And I did exactly the same for them! My best friends and closest confidantes are the men in that group. I am forever grateful to Henry,

Leonard, Mike, John, Dick, Russell, and so many other men who were part of my original I-Group. We long ago agreed that we were "friends for life, no matter what." What a great gift!

This support is so important to me that the first thing I did when I recently moved to the San Diego area was to find another I-Group there. I am really delighted and very lucky to have found a group near my Vista, California, home. Dave, Arturo, David, Stu, Patrick, and Art are my new circle of support. My new group is open to women, too, so I have had the joy of working with wonderfully alive, aware women, as well. Kate, Jennie, Wendy, and Julie are a few of these amazing, and courageous women. Thank you so much, men and women!

It is in my I-Group that I most often get to seek regular, honest, direct feedback about my life, decisions, attitudes, and choices. I regularly and ruthlessly seek and trust the feedback I get from people in my life on a regular basis. I willingly get others' feedback on my unconscious (shadow) parts, as well as for help in decision making, by asking for feedback from family, friends, and my support circles. This can be done through formal processes, like hot seats, feedback loops, or feedback circles, or informally through conversations and check-ins. Gathering feedback is a vulnerable, yet courageous act and a powerful way to gain awareness of my unconscious parts and shadow beliefs, as well as helping chart my progress.

Getting feedback from people I trust is also a great way to get "reality checks" on my decisions and thoughts. I am often amazed at how clearly people very close to me can see through me. They know my story and my defenses, which allows them to cut through my self-deception to get to my gold and my truth. I am deeply grateful for having people like that in my life!

C. Shadow Mining

Another valuable way for me to heal, and a critical piece I keep in the forefront (and another reason why support groups are so important to my growth and development!) is to continue to work on what I call "Shadow Mining." What is "Shadow Mining"? It's keeping awareness of the importance to my growth of fiercely and resolutely seeking my shadows. It requires deep digging (mining!). What are "shadows"? Shadows are defined by famous nineteenth-century psychiatrist Karl Jung as "those parts of me of which I hide, repress and deny, have lost awareness of, or have lost access to." I include the "dark shadows" (the unkind, hurtful, or evil things I can do), as well as my "gold shadows" (the beautiful, talented, and amazing parts of myself I hide, repress, and deny). I do this as courageously and regularly as possible in three different, simple, and useful ways:

a. <u>Through asking for feedback</u>, as discussed in detail in "B" above.

b. <u>By noticing on whom I project my darkness</u>

and my gold. Therapists often invoke the phrase, "If you spot it, you got it!" What I mean by this is I often notice parts of myself being reflected (or mirrored) back to me from others. If I have some quality, behavior, or belief that I don't like in myself, it often shows up as disliking that behavior, belief, or quality in another person— sometimes intensely. Likewise, if I see beautiful talents or gifts or expressions from another person that I admire or aspire to, they are also mirroring to me parts of my "golden shadow"— the wonderful and beautiful parts of myself I hide, repress, and deny. So those people I put on a pedestal can show me my own magnificence that I have been taught to bury and/or deny. Paradoxically, it is our golden shadows that are most often more difficult to become aware of, to dig up, and to reclaim!

The following powerful quote (one of my favorite quotes of all time!) clearly shows the paradox that mining my golden shadows is more difficult than mining my dark shadows:

"Our deepest fear is not that we are inadequate.

Our deepest fear is that we are powerful beyond measure.

It is our light, not our darkness, that most frightens us.

We ask ourselves, who am I to be brilliant, gorgeous, talented and fabulous?

Actually, who are you not to be?

You are a child of God.

Your playing small does not serve the world.

There's nothing enlightened about shrinking so that other people won't feel insecure around you.

We are all meant to shine, as children do.

We were born to make manifest the glory of God that is within us.

It's not just in some of us; it's in everyone. And as we let our own light shine, we unconsciously give other people permission to do the same.

As we're liberated from our own fear, our presence automatically liberates others."

Marianne Williamson from her book, *A Return to Love*, p. 165

Notice the last sentence of Williamson's quote. This is a powerful confirmation to me of the basic tenet of the Seven Generation story. Powerful and moving words, indeed! Mining both my dark and gold shadows is a key way for me to grow and develop as a human being.

    c. <u>By being willing to become aware of my "intention versus my impact"</u> on other people.

Oftentimes my actions and words land on another person in a manner that is quite different from what I intended. Usually my impacts occur to people I am closest to. I'll bet you have had that experience, too! When that occurs, I have two choices: (1) I can ignore my impact, dismiss it, or blame it on the other person; OR (2) I can seek to understand how my unconsciousness impacted that person. By doing so, I become aware of parts of myself I am completely unaware of, like my privilege, my disdain, and my greatest gifts. Seeking to understand my impacts has lead to an amazing amount of personal growth as I became more and more aware of how my words and deeds "land" on another person. I find that people also trust me much more when I am willing to "own" my impacts and account for them. I'll share more of this important tool in my section on Multicultural Awareness below.

These are three powerful tools I have purposely invoked in my life as a way to mine my own shadows and untangle me from my "psychic octopuses." As I reclaim these vital parts of me lost through my early conditioning, abuse, and damaging messages about my person, I notice much greater and immediate access to my life energy, my full capacities, my creativity, and my joy. I also heal myself, and my family system, in profound ways both obvious and subtle.

D. Doing Transformative Process Work

In my judgment, transformation is the whole purpose of growth and healing. I even named my company Transformational Adventures, LLC. By "transformation," I mean moving from one way of being to another. Transformation accompanies a true shift in consciousness and awareness. In order for this to occur, in my experience, a person must couple deep emotional release with a truthful re-scripting of impactful life events. In other words, changing the stories that play, like CDs on repeat, over and over again in our minds. For many of us, these tapes, or what some call conditioning, seem like our reality: That's "just the way it is." To challenge our reality, to change our conditioning, and to rewrite those stories requires courage, persistence, and support. I have made it my life's work to transform myself continually as I work toward greater levels of awareness and deeper connection with my higher self. The tools I share below are effective ones I have used consistently to aid me in this task.

1. Psychodrama. I have found psychodrama work to be extremely helpful in reclaiming the truth of who I am. I have practiced this process most often in MKP circles with support from talented facilitators, as well as in my I-group. By setting up emotionally damaging scenes from my life and re-scripting them, I have found huge healing. I have let go of many messages about me that were damaging, limiting, or simply wrong. Messages like: "I am not good enough, smart enough, or talented enough to succeed." Or "My body is not my own. It exists to serve the needs of others." Or "God does not

love or accept me just the way I am." Or "My mother's love was conditional." Or "The best way to deal with life is through drug or alcohol abuse." And on and on! We all carry many such limiting messages, in my experience.

One way to powerfully heal is to confront these wrong, hurtful, limiting messages, which often are carried like a disease from generation to generation within families. By confronting these messages within myself, I not only heal myself, but I also heal generations of my family in both directions.

2. <u>Rebirthing and Other Breath Work Practices</u>. Another very powerful modality for healing is breath work. I am a Certified Rebirther[11] and have been using this powerful technique myself and with clients for over twenty years. Rebirthing is just one branch of the breath work tree. Kriya Yoga, Holotrophic Breath Work, and Yogic Fire Breathing are three other branches. I support all the branches and have experienced most of them, but I have a special affinity for Rebirthing.

The healing idea behind all breath work is to superoxygenate the body by breathing more deeply and more often than we normally do so that the extra energy created through the breath goes to heal the blockages or places where we are stuck. Using these techniques, energy is quickly increased far beyond what we need to just survive, and that excess energy is directed to where it is most needed. The blockages are literally and figuratively "blown out" by this process. I have experienced many profound shifts using this technique myself and have facilitated many transformations for clients using breath work. I am most grateful this technique is in my life and works so well!

A Breath Work Transformation

In 1990 I was struggling with feeling as if I didn't have any spiritual grounding. I felt lifeless and as if God or Spirit wasn't present in my life. As a result, I felt dead and somewhat depressed. My therapist at the time, Jim, was also a Rebirther. After doing traditional therapy with me, he suggested I do some breath work on this topic. As I began to breathe the connected breaths associated with Rebirthing, I soon felt that incredible flow of energy throughout my body, but it didn't feel relaxing or enlivening at all. Instead, I began to feel profoundly sad. I felt as if I was floating all alone in space, completely isolated from everything I held dear. It was beautiful and peaceful in a way, but very lonely and dead—just like my life felt at that time! Jim suggested I breathe right into that feeling, which I did. My breathing got stronger and stronger, and I felt intense pain in my neck and back as my body tensed up almost unbearably. "Keep breathing!" was Jim's entreaty (as always)! "Just keep breathing, Rick." So I did.

As I continued to breathe, I could feel the pressure build up in my energy field. The pain and tenseness worsened, as did the strong sense of sadness and isolation. Suddenly, incredibly, this profound awareness leaped into my consciousness: I wasn't alone at all. My God created these stars and this space ... and me! A huge release occurred simultaneously. Tears suddenly welled up and flowed freely down my face. What felt like isolation and aloneness was simply my own long-standing tendency to isolate myself from God, my family, and loved ones. God loved me ... profoundly! In fact, he cherished me and cared about my existence deeply. I felt this immediate and deep peace come over me, as well as intense joy.

Now tears of gratitude and joy coursed down my cheeks as I continued to breathe with ever-increasing bliss. My whole body relaxed, and my breath slowed to a very deep and peaceful state. As the tears flowed unabated, I said the affirmation to myself that came directly out of my work: "My God loves and cherishes me, and I am an important part of his loving universe." I began to sob now with huge, hot tears of gratitude. Wow! What a release and transformation. I was loved, cherished, and an important part of the universe! I felt my depression lift, my isolation magically disappear, and my connection to my God and my loved ones soar! After a time, my tears ceased, and I sank into a deep calm similar to how I feel after a really good meditation. My body felt totally relaxed, and all my pain simply went away. I opened my eyes after a time to see Jim smiling down at me. I noticed that the colors of the room and the trees and plants outside were somehow very different and brilliant. Inside, I also felt completely different ... and brilliant! I have no doubt that some major transformation had just occurred in me.

Breath work is a simple, safe, and painless process that works wonderfully. And I always feel great when through—safe, relaxed, held by the sacred, and feeling the healing releases that occur so regularly through the breath. I have experienced profound new ways of being through this process.

3. Re-Evaluation Counseling. Sometimes called "Co-Counseling," Re-Evaluation Counseling (RC)[12] is another healing modality I have been trained in and highly recommend. To access the healing of RC work, you need to first do their introductory training called "Fundamentals," which teaches the basic technique of co-counseling, as well as some useful theory behind how it works. Once completed, RC members have access to a wide range of trainings, all employing the basic RC technique of co-counseling. Co-counseling occurs when two people decide to share time together, taking turns deeply listening as distress is released. The goal of RC work is "emergence" into the golden, wonderful, empowered beings we were meant to be. I have gratefully employed the tools of RC work for many years now.

One very beautiful and attractive aspect of the RC organization is the multicultural aspect of their work. RC recognizes that different cultures have different and special messages to work on. Hence, RC offers many workshops to help people of difference discharge their distress at being different. For example, they offer workshops on "People of Color and Their White Allies" or "LGBT People and their Straight Allies," or workshops to combat Jewish Oppression, Oppression of Women, and so forth. I found this aspect of RC focus refreshing and attractive, as it spoke so clearly to a deep part of myself that wants multicultural connection and awareness. And, this aspect of RC work supports my next invaluable tool for transformation!

E. Multicultural Awareness Work.

Another very key part of my recovery is dedication to multicultural awareness by gaining cultural competency. I cannot live in a world where inequality and harsh judgment of people different from me goes unchallenged. This work takes the personal level awareness and interpersonal level skills I have learned through all my healing practices and broadens it to include the cultural realm, enlarging my influence and worldview, as well as putting my Mission to work on a world stage. I am grateful to VISIONS, Inc.[13] for the training and mentoring I have received over many years as I have strived to gain more awareness of my privileges. In fact, I am so grateful that I have worked to become a Consultant for VISIONS, Inc.

As I become aware of the places in my life where I have unearned privilege and the places where I am oppressed, I gain greater compassion for myself and others. I reclaim the many parts of me that have been belittled and oppressed by society. I also gain a greater capacity to understand and to become an ally to those in my life who face persistent and damaging oppressions on a daily basis. I often do this by reaching out to people who are different from me, reading and watching media on this topic, attending workshops, becoming socially active, engaging people in conversations about our "isms," and internally noticing when I dismiss or oppress people who are different from me.

Here's where the tool of "Impact vs. Intent" comes in so handy. Why? Because so many of my impacts are multicultural in nature. Specifically, I am unaware of how privileged I am, and when I brandish my privilege unconsciously, it impacts (often deeply) people different from me whom I care very much about. For example, I carry much privilege as a white man. It is assumed I'm in a store to buy something and not shoplift. Police don't see me as a threat. My children do not have to pay extra attention when driving in any neighborhood for the "crime" of "driving while white," and so on. When I am oblivious to these privileges in the presence of my Black and Latino friends, I can (and have!) regularly impacted them in ways that were very off-putting. On the other hand, if I am willing to do the hard work of owning and recognizing my white privilege, then I am drawn closer to my friends of color, who implicitly trust me much more readily.

For example, recently I went to a restaurant with three Black friends, two men and a woman from Maui who was acting as our host. It was ironic that we had just completed a multicultural awareness training for the Maui community. My friend, Vicki, approached the person taking reservations for dinner and asked, "How long a wait is it for a party of four?" The white female maître d' said, "Let me check with the cooks to get a more exact waiting time." When the maître d' returned, she walked right past Vicki and the two other Black men to speak to me and tell me how long the wait would be. She then asked me, "What name should I put on the list?" I immediately caught the "ouch" that had just happened to my Black friends! The maître d' had assumed that the only white guy in the group was the correct one to report to and to name on the list, a clear sign of my privilege. She had also acted as if my Black friends were not even in the room. I then pointed to Vicki and said to the maître d', "I believe that Vicki was the one who asked you to check the wait time, and her name should be the one you use." My Black friends were both surprised and moved that I caught this seemingly small impact on them. And my friends appreciated the way I addressed it, which was immediate and empowering and did not create any drama. I only wish I were so aware all the time!

People of difference in my life talk often about experiencing what they call, "Death by a thousand paper cuts." The constant small and large acts of racism, sexism, and heterosexism that occur to them almost every day! One of my great privileges as a white, heterosexual man is not to have to experience those "thousand paper cuts" each and every day of my existence. Similarly, I choose to become more aware of my "heterosexual privilege" and my "male privilege" and my "middle-class privilege." It's not easy work, but it is tremendously satisfying to deepen my relationships with all the wonderful people in my life who are different from me. And, to be clear, I mess this up often! Gaining awareness in this realm, like so many others, is a lifetime commitment.

My multicultural awareness work in the world has been transformational for me in a big way. I have become much more aware of parts of me of which I was simply not conscious—my entitlement, my privilege, and the "legs up" I was getting from our culture that I didn't even notice, nor acknowledge. As I worked on these issues, I found that my relationships with my friends of color, my LGBT friends, women, and other people with differences in my life deepened and became more trustful. And this was one of the biggest payoffs for doing this work! My world and relationships became so much richer and diverse! Even my relationship with my father, highlighted in my introduction, was vastly different once I was able to understand and accept his differences. Perhaps more importantly, I have become much more accepting and loving of my own differences—a large part of my multicultural work! And I find that if I'm not actively pursuing multicultural awareness, I easily slip back into my haze of privilege, which leads to me "ouching" people I care very much about … which I've done all too often throughout my life.

F. Developing and Living Fully in My Golden Shadow and Dark Shadow Missions

Finally, I choose to live my life as much as possible in alignment with my Golden Mission of Service. In doing so, I call on and align myself with the energy and forces of my Higher Power. My life purpose is clearly reflected in my Mission of Service. I regularly state my Mission as part of my daily practice and use it as a tool to evaluate my decisions and the direction of my life. I own my gold and honor my capacity to serve and change the world. I commit to putting my Mission out front even when it is difficult and inconvenient. (For a simple example, I sign all my emails with my name, contact information, and Mission statement.) I also keep my Dark Shadow Mission in front of me by saying it regularly and noticing when I am acting out of my dark shadow. I regularly seek opportunities to serve and share my Mission with others. I seek opportunities to live my Mission by doing service work for my organizations, my community, and my family.

I also love to facilitate processes by which people can discern their own Missions—both dark and golden. I have had the privilege of doing this on many men's trainings around the world, as well as in corporate and not-for-profit trainings. I have helped people in their teens to their eighties create their Mission statements. I find almost always that people, when given the opportunity to access their Missions and create clear, concise Mission statements, are moved deeply and really enjoy the process. I learned the particular Mission process I recommend in the ManKind Project. I am grateful for this teaching and the opportunity to hone my skill at facilitating Mission processes. So what constitutes an effective Mission?

Mission = Vision + Action

Whether we're talking about Dark Shadow or Golden Shadow Missions, the most potent missions have two main components to them: (1) a Vision and (2) an Action. To be most powerful, our Vision should be a picture of what the world could be like if everyone lived the beautiful life we all want for ourselves, our families, and others. Visions come out of our soul's need for love, safety, connection with our Higher Power, order, and peace. Each of our visions will differ because each of our souls have different needs. And each of our families carry different stories, wounds, and traumas. Many of our visions come from what our little boys or little girls lacked as a child. For example, if your childhood home lacked love, perhaps we crave a loving world. If alcoholism and chaos reigned in our world, peace and order may be our main vision.

Visions are also very sacred. A vision also connects us with the divine within us, the "axis mundi" or vertical axis that connects the heavens with the Earth through us. My Native American brothers and sisters often talk of acting as a sacred conduit from something far greater than us (Great Spirit) that flows through us to bless our families, our tribe, and the world. It is often the Medicine Man or Woman who acts most directly as that conduit, as our intermediary. The symbol of this phenomenon is an eagle bone. Eagle bones are very sacred to Native People as they are hollow and represent that sacred conduit or pipeline to the Great Spirit. A truly beautiful and moving metaphor, isn't it?

Here's the miracle of Mission work, in my judgment: By invoking a Vision that comes out of my childhood wounds, my deepest wound can become my greatest Gold! I believe that this is what the alchemists of the Middle Ages were really looking for—not changing actual lead metal into gold, but rather changing the "lead of our woundedness" into the "gold of our Missions"! Our shadows become an inspiring impetus for us to heal ourselves, and our family systems. This is another marvelous, moving, and miraculous transformation, in my experience.

For many people, having a vision is enough. I disagree heartily! Perhaps the following short poem will highlight why:

> *Vision without action is impotent*
> *Action without vision is dangerous and undirected*
> *But vision and action together create an unstoppable force to transform the world*
> *(Author Unknown)*

Are you aware of places or institutions in this world where there's lots of vision but no action to support it? Me, too! And can you think of places where there's plenty of action that doesn't seem to be guided by any clear vision? It's obvious, right? To be truly transformative, a mission needs both the vision and the action! If you think of those iconic people who are thought of as world changers (people like Gandhi, Martin Luther King, Mother Teresa, Harvey Milk, Nelson Mandela, and so many more), what they had in common was a powerfully articulated vision backed up with potent action. Dr. King didn't just talk about having a Dream, he spoke about it regularly, lead marches, went to jail, and then paid the ultimate price for his mission. And he effected massive change in race relations in the U.S. that still reverberates today. The same can be said for each of these visionaries. So, what is missing? An action, of course!

So, I've established the second piece of an effective Mission as "A powerful Action we can do every day to make that Vision a reality." Some of us, whether we're aware of it or not, are already doing our action through our careers or volunteer work. Perhaps we're an artist, musician, poet, teacher, or minister. If so, good for you! And some of us have actions that we have fantasized about: Someday I'm going to volunteer as a docent, or I'm going to write my novel, learn to sculpt, take guitar lessons, or become a Big Brother or Big Sister, and so forth.

Either way, our actions potentize our Missions by making them a reality each and every day we choose to live them. Our actions can be something simple like "smiling at everyone I meet," or something more complex, like creating a program to assist young gang-bangers in your city (like my dearest friend, Henry

Thurman, did in Kenosha, Wisconsin, for fifteen years)! It doesn't matter how big your action is, what is important is making a commitment to do that action each day in order to create just a little more of your beautiful vision in the world. Can you imagine if each of us committed to do Mission work, how wonderful this world could be?

My Golden Shadow Mission speaks to my Golden Shadow—the beautiful and generative parts of myself that I hide, repress, and deny. As Marianne Williamson stated so beautifully in the quote I shared above, it is this part of ourselves that is most difficult to find, appreciate, and own. This makes our Golden Shadow Missions so very important for our own healing and growth, as well as helping to heal seven generations of our family in both directions. Here's my Golden Shadow Mission, honed over many years of personal growth work:

My Golden Shadow Mission is to Create a Passionately Loving and Peaceful Planet by Fostering Safe, Sacred, Diverse Healing Circles.

This Mission has worked for me for several years now. I use it to guide my life decisions, as well as to inspire me to be a better man, partner, father, and leader. As I stated earlier, I make saying my Golden Shadow Mission part of my daily practice so that I can remind myself and commit to being in alignment with how I want to behave in the world each day.

My Dark Shadow Mission is just as important for me to know. It expresses my dark shadow—the judgmental, selfish, evil parts of me I hide, repress, and deny. It also has a clear Vision that expresses what the world looks like from my wounded, disempowered place. And my Dark Shadow Mission is also potentized by actions that I do every day. For the vast majority of us, our Dark Shadow Missions are the mirror image of our Golden Shadow Missions (examples below). Also, for most of us, our Dark Shadow Mission will feel more familiar. We often experience a "truth response"— perhaps a shudder or a smile—when we first speak it. But people also almost immediately know that they have lived their Dark Shadow Missions through most of their lives. It is our "default setting," the one to which we will return virtually automatically IF we're not vigilant! That's why I also state my Dark Shadow Mission to myself each morning—to remind me of the clear choice I have: I can choose to live my Golden Shadow Mission or my Dark Shadow Mission. The choice is mine, and if I do not consciously choose, guess which one takes precedence? Yes, the Dark Shadow Mission. Here's my Dark Shadow Mission, which was also honed from many years of personal work:

My Dark Shadow Mission is to Create a Passionately Hateful and Chaotic Planet by Withholding All I Have to Offer and Shaming All You Have to Offer.

Notice how my Dark Shadow Mission has a vision that is the direct opposite of my Golden Shadow Mission, while the actions are opposites too. By the way, I am really, really good at living both my Missions in the world! I am an expert at passionately loving and being peaceful, which creates those safe, sacred, diverse healing circles that I love so much, and which I have the privilege of facilitating so often. I am also great at creating chaos and hate by withholding and shaming others—just ask my former wives! Each day, the choice is mine as to which Mission I will feed. It is a daily practice to place my commitment and my energy in service to my Golden Shadow Mission. By doing so, Mission work transforms me, and my family!

One Man's Mission Story

A few years ago, I was leading an MKP training in Los Angeles. One of the participants was a psychiatrist from Beverly Hills, California. He was literally the therapist to the stars! Jim was quite challenging to work with because he was very smart, and he thought his formal training was far superior to what we were presenting to his group of twenty-five participants. Jim continually verbally challenged me and the leader team on what was being shared with the participants. His resistance was epic—and not at all unusual. We simply held Jim and his resistance and his lack of trust of the process throughout the weekend. It was clear that he was projecting onto me some version of, "You don't get to use your power to manipulate me." I was an apt "projection screen" for Jim's wound.

When we got to the part of the weekend where we help men craft their Golden Shadow Mission statements, I led that process. He again resisted and refused to write even a rudimentary mission. Then we went into our "Carpet work/Psychodrama Process," which powerfully helps men to heal a part of their story that prevents them from fully embracing and living their Missions to their depth. Jim, though initially reluctant, finally stepped in to do his work. He confronted a lifelong message that he had not been able to access nor heal using the more traditional methods he had been trained in. He became fully aware of a message his father had planted early on in his life that had left him feeling scared and skeptical of his power. I watched in joyful amazement as Jim reclaimed his power and the capacity to wield it in a safe and conscious manner. It was a wonderful experience to witness Jim's journey and see the incredible transformation as he completely engaged his full power and aliveness! (Jim's work was also confirmation of the deep "father wound" he was projecting onto me and other men on the leader team of the weekend. It was the genesis of his resistance and suspicion of our competency and motives.)

Soon after that process, the participants are lead through a Dark Shadow Mission process to complete their mission work. As I led this piece and talked about the power of having a Dark Shadow Mission, Jim suddenly became very activated. He stood up and spoke to the group in a passionate way, participating fully for the first time. He said, "Thank you for this piece. What I know from my training as a psychiatrist is that 'for every action, there is an equal and opposite reaction.' I could not buy into the Golden Shadow Mission until I knew what was on the other side of it!" Jim then tearfully shared, "My Dark Shadow Mission is to create a painful and powerless planet by shaming your power and hiding my power." We all reveled in Jim's beautiful and powerful Dark Shadow Mission in reverent silence for a moment. Then, spontaneously, Jim "flipped" his Dark Shadow Mission to create his Golden Shadow Mission in the moment, "My Golden Shadow Mission is to create a healed and powerful planet by blessing your power and radiating my power." Wow!

At that moment, it was clear that Jim was now totally brought into our process. His resistance was completely gone, and he was filled with such joy and power that he began to dance around the room like a crazy man while the other participants cheered him on joyously! I share Jim's story to illustrate the point that it doesn't really matter if we create our Golden Shadow Mission first and then flip it to create our Dark Shadow Mission, or the other way around. Either way, our two mission statements mirror each other. Thanks, Jim, for showing me this point, as well as for reminding me that resistance to healing only points to the very issue that we need to heal!

So there are five very powerful and effective processes or techniques that I highly recommend to help us transform ourselves. By regularly employing a meditative daily practice, participating in powerful and honest support groups, working with transformational process work, doing my multicultural work, and regularly accessing and activating my missions, I slowly but inexorably move toward becoming the man, father, lover, and man of service I was truly meant to be in this incarnation. And, by doing so, I help transform the seven generations of my family both forward and backwards. What are some more thoughts on how to further use the incredible philosophy of the Seven Generations story to heal yourself and your family? Read on, my friends.

http://www.SevenGenerationsStory.com/

Chapter 4 Exercises

Exercise 13: What forms of healing work call to you? What has worked for you? I invite you to journal on that topic and share a story or two of your own healing— and its impact on your life and your family.

Exercise 14: Do you have a Dark Shadow Mission? If so, what is it? How has that Mission worked in your life to keep you small and powerless? How has it hurt you and your family?

Exercise 15: Do you have a Golden Shadow Mission? If so, what is it? How has that Mission served your own healing? How has it guided your life in positive ways? You can download my free "Guide for Creating a Golden Mission of Service, a Dark Shadow Mission and an Affirmation" from my website:

www.SevenGenerationsStory.com

Exercise 16: Support for your meditation practice. To get a free MP4 recording of Rick's Guided Visualization/Meditation, please go to:

www.SevenGenerationsStory.com

Chapter 5

More on How to Use the Seven Generation Philosophy to Heal Both Yourself and Your Family

"We do not act alone. The antecedents of our actions go back to our ancestors—what they have done, what they have passed on to us in the way of sin and in the way of virtue. And the consequences of our actions go forward to our descendants."
Arthur H. King, Abundance of the Heart, p. 93

"We believe it would be impossible to heal ourselves without it affecting all of us. The healing would reach backward to our ancestors and forward to our descendants. Although we cannot actually "live" their experiences, we are the literal effect of the emotions which were trapped around these experiences. Until we heal the traumatic memory, it will continue to affect our children and our children's children by virtue of the fact that we continue to pass on the same traumatic memories from one generation to another."
Ranae Johnson, PhD

"The emotions that impact our genes come not just from the experiences we had in this life. We inherit the emotional patterns and beliefs (or stories) of our ancestors. Deeply embedded in our DNA, these ancestral stories influence us in ways we are not even aware of. We are not prisoners of our genetic heritage. Our genetic codes are flexible, not fixed. Through powerful, but simple, self-healing techniques we can reset our genetic codes and with them the stories of our life."

These quotes above once again reiterate the power of our Seven Generations healing to effect change in ourselves, our families, and even our genetic code. Don't these ideas make it even more important and urgent for us to demand our own healing? In Chapter 4 I outlined several useful and effective ways to heal that I have successfully used for my own healing, as well as for people I have worked with, over a long period of time. There are, of course, many others, as well. The purpose of this chapter is to more fully explore how you can harness healing tools such as those I detailed in Chapter 4 to more fully heal yourself and your family. Then in Chapter 6 I will show how we can use these tools and ideas to implement transformational change on the entire planet. Sound interesting? I think so, too! Let's go.

One of My Profound Healing Releases

I am the proud father of two wonderful daughters, the stepfather of another terrific daughter, and the grandfather of three very precious granddaughters. There are only female descendants in my family. I am delighted and content with that now, but back in 1990, I was not. Back then, I really wanted a son to mentor and to carry on the family name. Then my wife became pregnant with our third child. We were both immediately certain that this child was our son (just as we were certain the very instant we conceived both our daughters!). The pregnancy was difficult from the start as my wife was almost forty years old. Nevertheless, we were very excited about having a third child—and a son.

At just after three months of gestation, one evening in August 1990, I suddenly heard a scream from our bathroom. I ran to my wife to discover that she was hemorrhaging badly into the toilet. She was having a miscarriage, and she was in pain and afraid. I immediately called our doctor, and he advised me to get her to the emergency room ASAP. Then he asked me to "retrieve any remains in the toilet and bring them to the ER so they could see if any of the fetus" was still inside my wife.

I rushed to find a neighbor to watch our two daughters while we were gone. Then I reached into the bloody toilet and found an egg-sized mass of tissue. As I briefly held that tissue in my hand, I noticed the beginnings of my son's limbs and head, along with his placenta. I put this tissue in a baby food jar and rushed my wife to the hospital where they performed an emergency D&C to stop the bleeding and remove any remaining tissue from the pregnancy. My wife lost so much blood that she was at severe risk, so she received a transfusion and remained in the hospital overnight.

In dealing with that emergency and the aftermath, I did not have the time (or take the time) to reflect on this loss. I buried my grief in service to being present for my wife and daughters. And the next day I went back to my teaching job and my volunteer work in my workaholic way. We had not yet told our family or friends we were expecting, so no one really knew how to support us through this deep trauma.

Fast-forward ten months to June 1991. I had traveled 500 miles north to the boundary waters of Canada to participate in an international men's retreat called "Men, Wilderness and Soul" put on by my friend Joe Laur. On the first afternoon of our encampment, all seventy-five participants were in a circle around a clearing we had hewed out of the surrounding forest that morning. After a spirited check-in from every man there, Joe walked to the center of the circle, placed a deer skull on a stump, and asked men who felt moved to walk to the center of the circle and share whatever they needed to get present. Immediately, I felt myself fall into deep grief, and I knew that it was about the loss of my son, which I had avoided for almost a year.

I stepped forward first to claim the "talking skull." Before I could say a word, I was overcome by an incredibly crushing grief (which I am feeling even now, some twenty-four years later). I fell to my knees as seventy-four other men witnessed my profound grief. I began to sob uncontrollably for what seemed like twenty minutes as the circle bore silent witness to my pain. During that episode, I let go of the fantasy of having a son. I grieved his loss. I grieved the loss for my wife and daughters. I owned my deep love for this being who had not been allowed to come to consciousness on this planet. But most of all, I grieved the young father within me who had harbored such deep dreams of having and raising my precious son—the boy child I had so strongly longed for and was getting my heart prepared to receive just before he died.

The wracking sobs slowly subsided, and I was finally able to share with this loving and accepting circle what I was experiencing. I shared, for the first time, the horror of retrieving my beloved son's remains from that bloody toilet and holding him in the palm of my hand. I shared the trauma of almost losing my wife and of dealing with my very young daughters' terror at this incident. I shared how I had buried this grief deep within me since that day in order to be present for my family and how I had felt dead and depressed and lifeless myself for a long time. I looked around the circle to see tears flowing down the cheeks of many men in that sacred circle—both friends and strangers—as they empathized with my story. I felt almost complete and spent.

Finally, I stood silently in the center of that circle and took a very deep, cleansing breath. At that instant, I felt an amazing peace come over me, accompanied by an equally amazing sense of aliveness. I viscerally felt the blessing of God raining down upon me like a healing, cleansing shower. It instantly became apparent to me that, by sublimating my own grief in order to serve my family, I had created a dysfunctional situation within me that had invited deadness, depression, and an existence devoid of passion. And I had not turned to the many sources of support and succor that were ever present in my life.

A gestalt occurred where I became instantly and deeply aware that I was choosing to be fully alive—grief and all—in that moment. In fact, I was reminded that I could not choose which feelings I would feel. It was a package deal—either I embraced them all or I shunned them all! That meant if I wanted to fully feel my joy and my aliveness and my connection to my Higher Power, I also had to fully feel my grief, my anger, and my fear. I then turned to these beautiful men and proclaimed with a deep and unshakable conviction, "I choose to live fully! I am alive! I own my grief fully. I own all my feelings fully. I choose to live! I … AM … ALIVE!" The men in the circle then raised their hands to the sky in silent blessing for my powerful, transformative, healing realization. The transformation within me was palpable, real, and long-lasting. I feel it deep in my bones and heart today, some twenty-five years later.

To this day, I remain committed to being fully alive, to being passionate, and to feeling all my feelings to their depth! And I believe that through this process I healed what may have become a generations-long trauma story about the loss of a child. As Dr. Ranae Johnson stated above, "Until we heal the traumatic memory, it will continue to affect our children and our children's children by virtue of the fact that we continue to pass on the same traumatic memories from one generation to another." Amen to that! I also remembered that my mother had experienced three miscarriages that bracketed my birth, so that energy and grief of miscarriages was alive and well in our intergenerational connection. When I returned home from my week in the woods, I shared my awakening with my wife. She expressed similar feelings, so we planned a sacred ceremony where we "buried" our son with honor and dignity while expressing our love for him—and our loss. It was wonderful and healing for us both.

This story is one of so many other powerful transformations I have been privileged to experience or witness in others. Some were dramatic, like many of the stories I've shared in this book, while others were more subtle, like the following story about my youngest daughter, Heather.

A Family Meeting

It was a typical busy Saturday for the Broniec Family in the summer of 1992. We were house cleaning and attending to the myriad details it takes to run a household of four. All day we had been at work, and my wife and I had been "chipping" at each other out of our irritation, overwork, and frustration. Unkind words had been shared between us as we all worked to restore our house to order. The tension was thick. Suddenly, Heather, who was five years old and our younger daughter, came into the living room with our family "talking stick." She banged it loudly on the floor and waited for my wife, our other daughter, Erica, and me to stop what we were doing and pay attention to her. Then she looked us all in the eye and very confidently and forcefully said, "I am calling a family meeting upstairs [in our family meditation room] in two minutes." She then turned with the staff firmly in her hand and walked upstairs to await our arrival.

My wife and I looked at each other with amazement and some confusion. We both shrugged our shoulders, nodded to each other, and then also headed upstairs to see what our empowered young daughter had to share. When we were all seated and expectantly waiting for what she wanted to say, Heather looked at us rather sternly, but sadly, and stated, "Mommy and Daddy, you have both been talking in unkind ways to each other all day. That scares me and Erica and it makes me sad and I want it to stop—now!" Then big tears coursed down her sweet, cherubic cheeks. Wow! I felt instant shame and sadness—and also well chastened. One look at my wife confirmed she felt the same. Heather was absolutely correct; we were allowing ourselves to be irritated and unkind with each other, and it was affecting both daughters, not to mention our own moods. The entire household was paying the price. We had taught our daughters how important it was to feel and to express our feelings in healthy, functional ways; to use our words directly and cleanly and not in sideways manners. And here she was employing the very tools we had taught her in such a powerful and wonderful way! What a gift—and a not-so-gentle reminder of healthy, loving communication!

My wife and I both turned to Heather to acknowledge her tears and anger. We both apologized to each other for our behavior. Then we both apologized to Heather and Erica for ruining their day. Then we all had a good cry together as we hugged each other and expressed our deep love for each other. We talked about ways to finish the day's chores with more joy and connection, and I promised to take the family out for ice cream when we were all done. Heather suggested we put on some upbeat music while we worked. We did that and finished our work on a much more loving and fun note. And that ice cream tasted sweeter than usual!

I cannot imagine being so aware and empowered at five years old like Heather was. This incident is a microcosm of both of our girls' childhoods. As my wife and I worked toward our own growth and healing, we taught our daughters very different skills and awareness than we had received as children. Our daughters were taught to trust themselves and their perceptions and to speak up, even to adults, and obviously felt empowered to do so! I am very grateful for that change in my family story. Other impacts on generations of my family are highlighted further in my introduction.

According to my understanding of the Seven Generations story, it is this kind of deep, incremental change that slowly, yet inexorably changes a family's story—even its DNA. I feel very blessed to have seen this transformation occurring in my life, the lives of my daughters and granddaughters, as well as with the many hundreds of clients and people I have had the honor of working with.

Kent's Story

In 1974, I had started my teaching career. Even though my teaching was very much Mission driven, I yearned to give even more back to my community. So I joined Big Brothers and became a mentor for a fatherless thirteen-year-old boy named Kent. At that time, I didn't have a clue how to be a mentor and friend to a young boy, but I learned quickly that all Kent really needed was a sympathetic ear to listen attentively to his story, as well as someone to share some fun with. I soon learned that Kent—an amazingly cute, blond-haired, blue-eyed young man—was headed for trouble! He was smart, yet really hurting from his parents' divorce. His father had abandoned him (and his three siblings), and his mother struggled to support them.

Kent and I soon forged a strong bond as we met weekly to do simple, fun activities like going swimming together or taking a hike or going out to get pizza. He slowly opened up to me as he began to trust me more. In between our "dates" he would often call me just to talk or share some problem he was wrestling with. I quickly fell in love with this terrific young man. About two years into our connection, Kent began to experience lots of pain in his lower back area. He had been to doctors several times, but nothing showed up in the exams. One day he confided in me that the pain was getting really bad, so I talked to his mother, and she took Kent to a specialist at Children's Hospital in Milwaukee. It was there that they discovered a tumor the size of a grapefruit at the base of Kent's spine!

Kent, his mother, and I were all shocked and mortified at this diagnosis. How had Kent's doctor missed something so obvious? How could he have been asking for help for many months, only to hear that his pain was "all in his head"? Surgery was recommended, with the caveat that, since the tumor was so deeply entwined with his spinal nerves, Kent would most likely lose all sensation below the waist. He'd never walk again, and he would lose control of his bladder and bowels and his sexual function. For a fourteen-year-old, this was unthinkable. His mother was understandably a wreck. I found myself supporting her as much as Kent. The finest surgeon at Children's Hospital performed the surgery and, miraculously, thankfully, removed the entire tumor without damaging any of Kent's spinal nerves. This was truly a miracle. He had regained full function!

However, Kent's incision had to heal from the inside out, so he was confined facedown for a couple months to a special bed that could be flipped upside down several times a day until his wound healed completely. Being inactive and bedridden for that length of time at fourteen years of age was particularly tough! I went to the hospital most nights after school to be with Kent. Usually he was facedown, so I would lie on the hospital floor in his room and read to him or simply talk face-to-face. As an encouragement for him to heal and get through his ordeal, I promised Kent that I'd take him out west camping for a month the next summer, once he was released. We planned a weeklong rubber-raft trip down the raging Colorado River, backpacking in the

Rocky Mountains, and hiking in the five national parks of Utah. Kent had never been west of the Mississippi River and was very excited to plan his experience in the great outdoors of the western U.S. We both couldn't wait!

Sure enough, Kent healed completely and was released from the hospital in time for our trip. We packed up my pickup truck with a camper on the back and headed west. We did everything we had planned—and then some—and spent a glorious month traveling together and celebrating his miraculous recovery in the wide-open spaces of Colorado and Utah! It was truly wonderful!

We got back just in time for Kent to start high school at the same school where I taught. It was great seeing him daily at school, his smile a mile wide as he experienced his first taste of high school life as a freshman. We checked in with each other on a daily basis. He seemed to thrive in this atmosphere, and he seemed to have matured overnight—no doubt a consequence of his illness and recovery. There were no vestiges of his physical pain nor his previous emotional troubles.

Then one day in late September, just a month after Kent entered school, I got a frantic call from his mother. "Kent's had an accident on his motorcycle on the motocross course. Rick, he's dead! I can't believe it!" I was stunned and numb. How could he have survived his cancer so miraculously only to be killed in an accident just a few months later? It didn't make sense, but I didn't have much time to process this very traumatic turn of events because I was supporting Kent's mother and siblings and friends. His mother, knowing I was a licensed minister in my church at the time, asked me to preside over Kent's funeral, which I agreed to do. It was one of the hardest days of my life. I stepped onto the stage at Saint Joseph's Catholic Church to see well over 500 grieving family members and friends and fellow students. Many students were crying or even wailing. Kent's mother and siblings sat in the front, sobbing uncontrollably. The grief and disbelief in the church was overwhelming.

Somehow, I got through the service and the dark weeks after Kent's passing, but I slipped into a fairly deep depression. I felt lost and confused and abandoned by God. My life became colorless, like a black-and-white movie. None of this made sense. I dropped out of Big Brothers because the thought of taking on another boy was just too much. About six months after Kent's death, I knew I needed help.

I finally went to a therapist, Mike, to talk about my blocked grief. After hearing my story, Mike sat back soberly and said, "Wow, I don't know how you negotiated your feelings after such a traumatic experience. You clearly have a lot of resources, Rick. I see and feel your deep grief, but I also wonder if you are experiencing some anger. Is it possible you are angry at God for taking Kent in what seems like such a callous and confusing manner?"

I looked at Mike with confusion for a moment and then had a powerful, truthful response. "Yes!" I flashed. "I think you are right. I am angry at God. In fact, I am furious!"

"Good!" Mike said. "This is your way out of your depression, Rick. When you withhold your anger and sadness, depression almost inevitably follows!" He continued, "So expressing your grief and anger at God will go a long way toward helping you heal your pain. The next time we meet, I'm going to set up a safe way for you to express your anger and grief. I believe you'll find much healing in doing this."

That week, I pondered Mike's invitation. It seemed almost unthinkable for me, a long-time lay minister and teacher, to be so angry with God. Yet, I knew that Mike's words rang true. The next week, we met at Mike's office. We spoke briefly about what I was feeling and confirmed that my rage was right there, just beneath the surface. Mike then handed me a plastic bat and placed me on my knees on the floor in front of a stack of couch cushions. "OK, Rick, now's your chance to get some of your repressed anger out. I invite you to hit the cushions with the bat. Come straight over your head and focus your energy into the cushions. Keep your eyes open and speak directly to God while you're doing this. Allow yourself to say whatever comes into your mind. It's a safe place to do this. I'll coach you. Remember, this is just the callous, unloving part of God you're angry at." After a moment, Mike asked, "Are you ready? GO!"

I began to beat the pillows with the bat. At first, I was halfhearted. But with Mike's urging, I began to let more and more of my anger out. Suddenly, a dam broke within my heart, and I felt a huge surge of rage come out. I was hitting the cushions with all my fury while yelling loudly, "How could you do this to Kent and me, God? Where's your love and compassion? You have abandoned me!" I continued to swing. Then another level of rage bubbled up. "Fuck you, God!" I yelled. "Fuck you for taking Kent. Fuck you for abandoning me. Fuck you for your capriciousness. FUCK YOU!"

This anger process went on for about fifteen minutes and then suddenly and unexpectedly, I became overwhelmed with my deep grief. Another dam gave way and I began to sob uncontrollably. I dropped the bat and fell to the floor as Mike cradled me. After a long while, I was able to croak out, "I miss you so much, Kent. I am so sorry your young life was ended so abruptly. I love you." At that, a great peace came over me. I fell into a deeply restful place as Mike held me. I felt my love for Kent come up so strongly. And that's when I got in touch with the part of God that was unconditionally loving—even when I was furious with him/her. "I forgive you, God, for taking Kent. I don't fully understand why, but I feel your love now and am sorry for being so angry at you." I opened my eyes and felt completely different. I felt loved and cared for and peaceful and fully alive. I looked at Mike and said, "Thank you, Mike. I couldn't have done this without your guidance and support. I feel so much better."

Mike replied, "You're welcome, Rick. But you did the work—and good work it was! Now pay attention to your anger and grief as it will come up again and again in waves as you process this trauma. But know you are well on your way to healing, my friend."

I will never forget Kent, nor Mike's helpful intervention. A few months later, I felt called back to Big Brothers. Soon after that, I was paired up with David, another energetic, wonderful, fun, young eight-year-old boy. David and I worked together for over ten years until he graduated from high school. I was able to be there fully for David, in large part due to my work in dealing with my grief and rage and pain. David went on to college and a very full and fulfilling life. I'm glad to have had a positive influence on his growth and development, and that of his family! Another incredible example of how the Seven Generations story has worked in my life.

Greta's Story

In 1974 I was a first-year chemistry teacher at Case High School in Racine, Wisconsin. Greta was a fourteen-year-old freshman in my homeroom who sat in the front row. We chatted briefly each morning as we met for announcements and prepared for a busy day at school. I discovered that Greta was a German immigrant whose parents spoke little English. She was very shy and quiet, but she responded well to my morning banter and friendly energy, even though I rarely saw her smile. She spoke to me once about feeling frustrated with her very strict German parents and her sense of isolation from any kind of social life. I understood that her home life was very austere and that she did not feel valued or loved by her parents as they struggled with survival in a country so different from Germany.

One day, well into the year, Greta was absent. This was highly unusual for her, but I thought little of it. The next day, she was back in class, but I noticed she seemed very distant and sad—and that she was wearing a long-sleeved sweatshirt on an eighty-degree day. Then, when she reached for a paper I was handing out, I noticed she had bandages on both wrists. Somehow I knew instantly what had happened: she had attempted to slit her wrists the day before, had survived her suicide attempt, and simply came back to school the next day like nothing had happened!

I didn't say anything to Greta about my observations then, but I went to talk to her school counselor right after homeroom about what I suspected. Later that day, the counselor sought me out to tell me that Greta had, indeed, attempted suicide, that she had agreed to start regular counseling, and that her parents, completely unaware of these events, had agreed to attend Greta's counseling sessions as well. I was relieved to know that Greta was getting the help and support she needed and soon forgot about the incident. Greta and I never spoke of it, and she went on to graduate high school and go on to college.

Now fast-forward thirty-three years to 2007. I was still teaching chemistry at Case High, heading for retirement at the close of the year. I was having my last round of parent-teacher conferences in April and had my usual line of involved parents filling my classroom, checking in with how their students were doing. At the end of a long evening, the last parent in line came forward to greet me. I did not recognize her until she spoke to me with her slight German accent. "Mr. Broniec, do you remember me? I am Greta, and you were my homeroom teacher over thirty years ago." I immediately knew who she was, but I had no idea why she was in line since I did not have any of her children in class.

Greta added, "I have been wanting to speak to you for a long time and realized that with your retirement, this may be my last chance." I waited expectantly as she continued. "I never shared with you before how deeply grateful I am that you noticed me and my situation around my suicide attempt so many years ago. You were so kind and gracious and got me the help I so desperately needed at the time. You never judged me or even mentioned the incident again." Then Greta took a deep breath and began to cry. "What I want you to hear is my profound gratitude for the man and teacher you are. I want you to know that I am here today, alive, only because you took notice of my pain and compassionately reached out to help. I also want you to know that I have a good life now. I am happily married to a wonderful man and have two beautiful children going to this very school. I graduated from nursing school and have been an RN here in town for twenty-eight years. None of this would have happened without your intervention. You see, back then I was determined to finish the job the next night, believing that no one cared for me. But your help, along with that of the school counselor, saved my life. I went into therapy with my parents, and we worked some things out. None of the good things in my life would have occurred if you hadn't simply noticed my call for help. Finally, I want you to know that I am determined to pay back your gift by helping other kids in our community. I volunteer for Big Sisters now in your honor, working with a motherless girl each week. That's part of your legacy that I think you should know."

At this point, Greta stopped talking and reached out to hug me, and we were both crying in joy at the miracle of Greta's healing and the wonderful life she had lived. We hugged each other for several minutes as we shared this very intimate and precious time together. I was filled with profound gratitude myself to have received this beautiful, unexpected gift. Greta was mirroring to me a piece of my healing influence on her, her family (and the world) in such a meaningful way. After a while she said, "Well, I am so glad I had the chance to thank you in person, Mr. B!"

I responded, "Greta, it is I who should be thanking you for sharing your story with me. I would never have known my impact on your life if you hadn't been gracious enough to share your story with me. This sharing puts my entire career in a different perspective.

I'm so proud of you and what you've accomplished and given back! Thanks so much for coming in!"

At that point, Greta and I hugged briefly once more, and, smiling broadly now, she left. I sat down at my desk for a few moments and felt extreme joy and gratitude course through me as I pondered the sweet encounter with my former student. More tears rolled down my face as I realized how my own awareness and healing had helped me serve a young person in her time of real need. And my simple act had rippled through her family and the world in wonderful ways that I could not have suspected. Life is truly amazing!

Once again, I had strong evidence that my own healing work had influence not just on myself and my family, but on others' families as well. Let's take a look at how we can extend the Seven Generations story to help heal the planet. There's modern awareness and technology emerging that strongly corroborates this ancient aboriginal philosophy—and great, newer tools to access! Are you ready?

http://www.SevenGenerationsStory.com/

Chapter 5 Exercises

Exercise 17: Share a story where you have helped another person. How has your own healing impacted your ability to be present for another? What impact did your help have on that person and his/her family?

Exercise 18: Where might your feelings and energy be blocked? What feelings are you withholding? Where can you go to get support in releasing these feelings in a healthy way?

Exercise 19: Where have you made a positive impact on your family, community, or the world? How does that feel? How might you continue exercising that positive influence?

Chapter 6

Hope for the Planet: Implementing Seven Generations Healing in the World

"In order to heal or change your life you must first discover the underlying, often unknown, limiting beliefs you may be holding on to. You must find the ... story handed down from your ancestors through your genes that has created the interference pattern in your DNA and that is causing the ... disturbance in your physical or emotional world."
Margaret Ruby, The DNA of Healing, p. 19

"A particular pattern will continue to run in a family until the pattern is broken or resolved. Unfinished business from an ancestor can affect our lives and actually show up in our DNA and the eyes. As we release unprocessed emotions, we are not only healing our lives but also the pain of untold generations as we give that gift to our descendants."
Ranae Johnson, PhD, Reclaim Your Light Through Rapid Eye Movement, p. 62

"When we look closer at the Orders of Love [a concept of Constellation Therapy], we enter a realm that is beyond traditional psychotherapy, and initiates a movement over the threshold into the dominion of the Soul. ... At the heart of the Soul is the acknowledgment and acceptance of what is. This is the basis and power of love."

John L. Payne, The Healing of Individuals, Families and Nations,
p. 2

In 1994 I felt called to receive some training in Family Constellation Therapy. I went to several workshops in the Milwaukee area and participated actively in healing processes led by our facilitator, who was, at that time, the only Family Constellation therapist in the state of Wisconsin. I became hooked on the process and have been very privileged to have received training in Family Constellation Therapy from several different practitioners over the years.

I initially came into Family Constellation work somewhat skeptical, as I had been highly trained in psychodrama and gestalt, had done years of traditional therapy, and had seen many miraculous healings take place using these tools. But Family Constellation was quite different from psychodrama and other modalities in that no words and a very minimal story were shared with participants in a constellation. Instead, they were expected to tune into the "Knowing Field" that, I was taught, was present in every family and nation and culture that contained wisdom, truth, and knowing that reached across generations. That "Knowing Field" is always present and can be accessed, according to the teachings of Family Constellation Therapy, quite easily by a person taking on a role in a constellation to gather information about the person's family not previously known consciously. This is very similar to the thinking contained in the Seven Generations story.

I have found amazing confluences between the Seven Generations story and the teachings and theory behind Family Constellation Therapy. I see these two philosophies as being mutually consistent and supportive. And I am grateful to have been exposed so deeply to both ways of thinking. I see Family Constellation work as a modern tool that is useful to further empower and enact the ancient Seven Generations story—a "both/and" rather than an "either/or" scenario. In my opinion, they complement each other perfectly. I understand these two healing philosophies, coming from very different sources, to be different facets of the same gem, coming from the same Source.

What is Family Constellation Therapy?

Family Constellation Therapy, founded fifty years ago, is a mode of healing that accesses family stories believed to be held in the DNA and "morphogenic field" (also called the "Knowing Field") of a family, culture, or nation. The therapy was invented by German citizen Bert Hellinger, a former Anglican priest who worked with the Zulu tribe in South Africa for twenty years. He synthesized features of gestalt, psychodrama, psychoanalysis, primal therapy, tribal thinking, and many other traditions into what has come to be known as Family Constellation Therapy. This therapeutic process has been widely accepted in Europe, but is less well known in the U.S. Practitioners of Family Constellation Therapy claim that a person's present-day problems and difficulties may be influenced by traumas suffered in previous generations, even if those who are affected are not aware of the precipitating event or trauma in the past. These traumas include early deaths of family members, murders, rapes and sexual assaults, miscarriages, abortions, and other acts of violence.

According to the website of the Hellinger Institute of Northern California, "A Family Constellation is a three-dimensional group process that has the power to shift generations of suffering and unhappiness. Bert Hellinger, the founder of this work, who studied and treated families for more than 50 years, observed that many of us unconsciously 'take on' destructive familial patterns of anxiety, depression, anger, guilt, aloneness, alcoholism and even illness as a way of 'belonging' in our families. Bonded by a deep love, a child will often sacrifice his own best interests in a vain attempt to ease the suffering of a parent or other family member.

Family Constellations allow us to break these patterns so that we can live healthier, happier, more fulfilled lives. In a moment of insight, a new life course can be set in motion. The results can be life-changing."[16]

In the words of Bert Hellinger, the founder of this therapeutic technique, "When there has been a trauma or someone in the family system has been excluded, forgotten, cast out, or suffered a difficult fate, someone of the following generations unconsciously and invariably will step in and bring the lost member's destiny back through living it out in this lifetime effecting us in ways in which we have no understanding. It happens out of a deep but hidden loyalty out of the secret law that will not allow anyone of a family system being denied the right to belong. It is a love so deep that the family member may unconsciously choose to die, rather than 'betray' the family bond."[17] So our loyalty and caring for our family members, along with our deep need for belonging, bring us to the point of even hurting ourselves to support other members of our family. Again, there are many features of Family Constellation Therapy that mirror many of the beliefs of the Seven Generations story. Let's continue this exploration.

What is a Family Constellation?

A constellation is set up to reveal previously unconscious events or traumas, or the effects of these traumas, in our family's story and DNA. The belief is that our family stories and traumas are passed down from one generation to another through our DNA by this "Knowing" or "Morphogenic Field." In an attempt to truly love our parents and grandparents, according to Hellinger, we take on the burden of these traumas (usually unconsciously) in order to maintain the "Order of Love" within our family system and to belong.

"Accessing the Morphogenic Field, Systemic or Family Constellation Work operates to reveal deep and healing resolution through an intimate experiential process and may be done in a private consultation, telephone constellations or most often in a group workshop setting. In addition to Bert Hellinger's 'Orders of Love,' we are working with the morphogenic, or 'knowing field.' This field, as identified by biophysicist Rupert Sheldrake, as the place which holds the record or information pattern of our entire family system, is similar to the way in which we inherit the DNA structure from our forebears. This energetic informational field 'knows' the deep down realities of the family system and contains not only the deep-seated wounds, but the mode of healing, as well."[18]

In addition, this system of healing believes that our deepest need is to be seen, acknowledged, and belong. "This deep longing for belonging guides our life. As part of the family, everyone has the right to belong. Even though we live in such individualistic times, the soul still honors the realities of the tribe. We like to believe that we can choose whom and what to acknowledge, and what not. It is possible, but the price will have to be paid, usually by later generations. The family soul does not rest until every member and event is fully included again."[19]

A Family Constellation Process

In my very first Family Constellation workshop, I observed and participated in a healing constellation where we were attempting to support Jane, who was finding it difficult to have satisfying connections with men—both emotionally and sexually. Jane seemed to have placed her father on a very high pedestal and was equally angry, judgmental, and distant from her mother. Since both Jane's parents had passed on, it was difficult for her to get resolution with her parental issues in a traditional psychological therapeutic setting, so she came to a Family Constellation workshop to explore the dynamics of her confusion about her parents, in an attempt to understand why she was still having trouble connecting with men in meaningful ways after years of personal work.

Ron was our practitioner and workshop leader who facilitated the process. Jane placed her father and mother into the constellation on a twelve-foot square of carpet in the center of the room. Immediately, the two people standing in for Jane's mom and dad moved as far apart as they could on the carpet, and they turned their backs to each other. This caused some consternation for Jane, as her father was a highly respected minister in her hometown and to whom she felt very close. She was aware of long-standing tension between her parents, but she couldn't understand why this had occurred. Jane filled us in on her deep respect for her father. "He was a loving man who practiced service in a big way throughout his church and community. He even bought an apartment building in town and created an organization to serve homeless, unmarried mothers and their children, so they had a safe and inexpensive place to stay."

Ron asked a participant to stand in for Jane. That

participant migrated across the carpet to stand near her father, looking at him face-to-face. Then Ron added another figure on the carpet to represent the women who had lived in the apartment building. That person spontaneously moved away from Jane's father and mother and took a position kitty-corner to both, but looking toward her father. Once the constellation had been arranged, Ron asked the "stand-ins" to speak.

Immediately, the person representing Jane's mother said angrily, "You think your father is so holy. You don't know that he regularly went to that apartment building to have sex with several of these women! He did this for years and shut down any intimacy with me."

Her father stand-in then stated, "That's true, but I did it because you didn't seem to want to be intimate with me after Jane's birth, and that was very painful."

Jane instantly began to weep uncontrollably. The very uncomfortable truth about her father's (and mother's) behavior, seemingly summoned out of the ether, suddenly became impossible to ignore or rationalize away. Jane's "truth response" was unmistakable and poignant. She was instantaneously forced to confront her previously uncritical and totally loving and accepting view of her father and to feel the startling truth of what the mother stand-in had shared. She was also compelled to reevaluate her harsh judgments about her mother and find some empathy and understanding for her. Suddenly, the "story" that her mother was cold and unloving toward both Jane and her father, causing the rift between them, changed virtually instantly! She suddenly found compassion for her mother, who had kept this damaging and very painful "family secret" for many years to protect her father's reputation, legal status, and livelihood. Jane realized that her mother had shown both Jane and her father love by holding this painful secret as best as she could. Jane suddenly knew her mother to be a very loving woman!

Jane also had revelations about her seeming inability to connect with men. Suddenly, she was aware that her inordinately close relationship with her father, along with the rejection and judgment of her mother, put her in a place where she was inappropriately bonded to her dad—so close that no other man could "get between" them to bond with her in a healthy manner. Jane realized that she had become her father's "surrogate wife" and was inappropriately emotionally bonded to him to the exclusion of any relationships she tried to initiate with other men. This revelation was both difficult for her to accept, as well as very relieving, as it gave her a more complete story about her family lineage. Jane completed her process with a peaceful demeanor and a smile on her face. Clearly some deep healing had occurred within her. She expressed her gratitude to the group for their support in uncovering this previously unknown dynamic in her family system.

Family Constellation practitioner, Berthold Ulsamer states, "Children seldom or never dare to live a happier or more fulfilling life than their parents. Unconsciously they remain loyal to unspoken family traditions that work invisibly. Family Constellations are a way of discovering underlying family bonds and forces that have been carried unconsciously over several generations." It seems clear that Jane was living her life by that principle previous to her healing process. I wonder how many of us are loyal to our ancestors to the extent that we have unconsciously sacrificed our own happiness?

My Own Family Constellation Healing Process

Soon after I started working with Family Constellation Therapy, an issue in my own life surfaced that was holding me back. I decided to bring it to my next Family Constellation workshop. The issue was about my mother's side of the family and their relationship to each other and our church, which was getting increasingly hard for me to ignore. I stepped out on the carpet first during this weekend workshop and shared briefly that my mother and her two older brothers, George and Greg, had a rocky relationship that impacted me because I was active in the church that George ran and all of us attended.

Ron placed people to represent my mother and her two brothers out on the floor, as well as a representative for me. Immediately, my two uncles moved across the carpet from my mother. She instinctively turned away from her oldest brother, George, the head minister of our church. My representative walked to the opposite corner between my mother and uncles and looked away from the scene. Ron asked my mother's rep, "What's going on here?"

She replied, "My father has had such an impact on us that we are having a hard time trusting each other." My grandfather was a prominent preacher in Zion, Illinois. He was a hands-on healer in the 1930s and '40s and was quite famous. He also demanded from his children that they live in a very austere and religiously repressed manner, which my uncles resented deeply.

Ron then picked a rep for my grandfather. He walked to the center of the carpet and raised his arms toward his sons, but they did not respond. Ron turned to my mother again and said, "Now what is going on?"

She responded, "I looked up to my father very much, and still do, but he never told me or them that he loved us. They turned away from him and have never forgiven him for giving all his attention and love to his parishioners and none to them. However, I understood and have forgiven him. My father was a saint!"

Ron then turned to the representative for my mother's oldest brother. "What is happening for you?"

"I am very angry at my father. He never told me he loved or respected me. He never loved my mother, either. I disappointed him no matter what I did. I was never holy enough for him. I hate that my sister has him on a pedestal! I am angry with her and do not trust her. Now I am running a church, but I am just as intolerant as my father—especially toward my sister and her family."

At that, the rep standing in for me began to cry hard. "What's going on for you?" asked Ron.

My rep responded, "I always looked up to my uncle George. He always took me in when my mom and dad were having difficulty. But his intolerance and anger at having to serve parishioners, along with his gossip behind their backs, led me to not trust or respect him anymore. I don't think it is possible for me to work with him in this church or support his behaviors anymore."

After a moment of silence, my rep then continued unexpectedly. "I believe that my mom, my uncles, and my grandfather were all quite mentally ill. Their schizophrenia is mild, but very evident, and I need to get away from their influence." My mother's younger sister had indeed been diagnosed with mental illness and shot herself in the head in my mother's kitchen in 1953, evidence that the entire family carried this gene!

I had an immediate "truth response" to this statement. That was the truth I was avoiding: There was long-standing mental illness in my mom's family, and I had to leave the only church I had ever attended, along with the ill family members who ran that church! This was a very scary proposition for me, as my whole world had revolved around my church; everyone I socialized with—my friends, my family, and my wife—all were members of this church! I also realized through this process that my mom was hopelessly enamored with her father and could never acknowledge the damage his hyper-religiosity and inability to love his children did to her. I saw that my mom and her brothers were all really damaged and would not seek any healing under the guise that "God would heal them."

I knew I had to leave the organization, an organization for which I ministered for twenty years, sat on the board of directors, and acted as treasurer for eighteen years. It was one of the hardest things I've ever done, but soon after this Family Constellation weekend, I resigned my positions from the church and left that organization. While it was very difficult, I am now quite clear that this was the best thing I could do for myself. I took with me the deep spirituality I had practiced there, but I left behind the family dysfunctions and intergenerational traumas I now saw so clearly! And I found a deeper and much healthier social circle outside my church that serves me to this day. I am so grateful to Family Constellation Therapy for helping me have this realization and leading me to another invaluable transformation.

That process also reminded me, yet again, of the familial, intergenerational aspects of traumas passed down so predictably from one generation to another. Whether viewed through the lens of Family Constellation Therapy or the Seven Generations story, I can see clearly that several generations were impacted by traumatic events in my family's history that, unless they are healed, will continue to bedevil generations of my family. Now that I know this fact, it is incumbent on me to work to heal these familial, intergenerational wounds so that my ancestors, my descendants, and I can be freer and healthier.

I believe that Family Constellation Therapy is doing a great service to the planet by institutionalizing the concept of intergenerational or familial healing. By offering the healing techniques of constellations, this organization is blessing the world by bringing into the light previously unsuspected traumas that persist for generations within family systems, unless they are consciously healed!

I end this chapter with this poignant quote by Sarah La Rosa: "We hold space when we hold the container steady so that the contents can be taken out and examined by whoever needs to examine them. We did not create those contents, nor the container itself. We are merely the bearer—the stabilizer who uses our muscle to heft its weight up to allow for easier access— whether by another or ourselves. When holding space, it is neither our job nor our right to interpret the meaning of the contents. To do so is a violation of the others' journey, and our own."

Holding space for transformation and healing is exactly what Family Constellation Therapy does, in my experience! I believe that we can move beyond healing ourselves and our family to helping heal the planet by using the awareness and the tools of Family Constellation Therapy! Using these tools gives me hope that this awareness can heal wounds beyond me and my family—to cultural wounds and the deep, intractable issues that plague our world. In doing so, the traumatic and lasting effects of war, genocide, racism, and the other "isms" can be healed. I firmly believe this, and that belief activates both my Golden Mission, as well as my own healing process. It gives me tremendous incentive to continue on this healing path. I hope it does the same for you too, my friends!

http://www.SevenGenerationsStory.com/

Chapter 6 Exercises

Exercise 20: What awareness have you gained about your family's story that may not have been spoken out loud? Journal this story and share it with another person.

Exercise 21: What are some of your family's generational traumas that might be healed using the technique of Constellation Therapy? How have these family stories/traumas influenced you and your sense of well-being?

Exercise 22: What world problems do you see being healed by work such as Family Constellation Therapy and such awareness of the Seven Generations story? Is there a particular issue that calls to you to help with? How does that feel?

Conclusion

"You are never alone, even during what you think are your weakest moments. You have thousands of years of powerful ANCESTORS within you, the blood of The Divine Great Ones in you, supreme intellect and royalty in you. Infinite strength is always on tap for you. Know that!"
Author Unknown

"We believe it would be impossible to heal ourselves without it affecting all of us. The healing would reach backward to our ancestors and forward to our descendants. "
Ranae Johnson, PhD

My friends, I am grateful that you have read thus far. I hope that, like me, you are inspired to dive into some of the techniques I have recommended for you to heal. Do it for yourself, and do it for your family and the planet. I continue to do my own work regularly and as deeply as I can. I have noticed huge changes in my life ... and in the lives of my family members and the many thousands of people I have had the privilege of working with over the years. I believe I am becoming the "man I was meant to be on this planet." That feels so very good!

I firmly believe the Seven Generations story! I believe that there's tremendous value in thinking about my family as seven generations in the future and seven more into the past. I believe that as I do my work, my family's story changes and heals. I believe that the dysfunctional threads, traumas, and pain that bedevil my family—and most others—can be healed. I believe in doing so, my familial DNA can change, benefitting my family well into the future, as well as the past.

I invite you to employ powerful tools like starting your daily practice, working with support groups, diving into shadow mining, doing transformational process work, developing multicultural awareness, and exploring your Golden and Dark Shadow Missions to transform your life, your family, and this planet, which is in such dire need for healing.

I also invite you to explore the amazing realm of Family Constellation Therapy as another important arrow in your quiver of healing. Seek workshops and facilitators that call to you, knowing that your work benefits far more than just yourself.

Finally, please know that you are not alone! Know that your ancestors support you and that you have "infinite strength," as our quote above assures. Know also that you will attract to yourself other allies, other teaching, and other healing work as you dive into your own healing process. Know that I am one of those allies ... and that I need your support too!

Why wait? Start today! And if you have already started, I invite you to rededicate yourself to your learning, growth, and healing. Make it a priority, my friends! If you don't do this for your family, who will? If you and I don't do it for the planet, who will? As Dr. Ranae Johnson states so clearly in her quote above, "We believe it would be impossible to heal ourselves without it affecting all of us. The healing would reach backward to our ancestors and forward to our descendants." Isn't that incentive enough to dive deeply? I think it is. My 'amazing' granddaughter, Jaida, believes it is. I hope you do, too. Let's do this together.

In Gratitude

I would be so grateful if you could take a minute or two to share what you loved about *Seven Generations Story* and provide an honest review on my Amazon sales page.

The Seven Generations Story

About the Author

Rick Broniec, MEd. is a professional Keynote speaker, writer, coach and leadership workshop facilitator. He is a member of the National Speakers Association. Rick taught International Baccalaureate Chemistry in an urban public high school for 35 years and is recognized as a "Master Teacher" through entry in the SE Wisconsin Educator's Hall of Fame. Rick has been honored with a number of national awards, including The Presidential Award for Excellence (from President Ronald Reagan), the Kohl Award and the Tandy Award.

n addition, Rick has worked in the leadership training and personal growth field for more than 30 years as an author, speaker, workshop leader, leader trainer and multicultural awareness trainer. Rick is certified as a Full Leader and Leader Trainer for the ManKind Project International (MKPI) since 1992, leading well over 160 trainings for that not-for-profit men's organization. Rick is also a leader in multicultural work for MKPI and has lead over 40 Multicultural Awareness Workshops around the globe. Rick's first book was *"A Passionate Life: 7 Steps for Reclaiming Your Passion, Purpose and Joy"* (available in hard copy or on Kindle).

Rick resides in Vista, CA. He is the father of three wonderful daughters and the grandfather of three spectacular granddaughters, his greatest teachers. When Rick is not working, he enjoys riding his Harley Davidson motorcycle, camping, golfing and reading voraciously.

About Rick's Business

Rick Broniec, MEd. is the Vibrant Relationships Guy. His business, Transformational Adventures, LLC. is focused on creating and supporting vibrant, authentic relationships in the workplace and at home. Besides writing books, Rick reaches his audience through keynote speaking, transformational coaching, powerful leadership training, blogging and multicultural awareness training. Rick's particularly enjoys working with individuals and groups on Passion, Purpose, Mission and Authentic Appreciation.

Rick travels extensively internationally and across North America to bring his message to thousands of people each year. To book Rick for a Keynote address, a workshop or for coaching, please contact him through his website: www.vibrantrelationshipsguy.com Rick is a member of the National Speakers Association.

Connect with
Rick Broniec, MEd.

Websites:

www.sevengenerationsstory.com/

www.vibrantrelationshipsguy.com/

Email: rick@sevengenerationsstory.com

Social Media:

Facebook: www.facebook.com/rick.broniec

LinkedIn:
www.linkedin.com/profile/view?id=13236662&trk=hp-identity-name

Twitter: twitter.com/rbroniec

Pinterest: www.pinterest.com/rbroniec/

Endnotes

1. Tim Blueflint, from his website *Shades of the Rez*.

2. Oren R. Lyons, from "Seven Generations Sustainability" in *Wikipedia*.

3. Seventh Generation, Inc. seventhgeneration.com

4. The International Council of Thirteen Indigenous Grandmothers, www.grandmotherscouncil.org/ See also: Wikipedia entry with same title. And: http://www.grandmotherscouncil.org

5. "For the Next Seven Generations," Documentary found at www.forthenext7generations.com/

6. Sister Jose Hobday, "Seventh Generation Sustainability," *Wikipedia*.

7. Dr. Judith Rich, "Healing the Wounds of Your Ancestors," *Huffington Post*, April 27, 2011.

8. ManKind Project can be found at www.mkp.org

9. Rick Broniec, Med., *A Passionate Life: Seven Steps for Reclaiming Your Passion, Purpose*

and Joy, Create Space, 2011. Available on Amazon.com

10. Ted Andrews, *Animal-Speak: The Spiritual & Magical Powers of Creatures Great and Small*, Llewellyn Worldwide, Minneapolis, MN, 1993.

11. Jamie Sams and David Carson, *Medicine Cards: The Discovery of Power Through the Ways of Animals*, Bear and Company, Santa Fe, NM, 1988.

12. Re-Evaluation Counselling can be found at: www.rc.org.

13. VISIONS, Inc. can be found at: www.visions-inc.org

Bibliography

I have found the following sources of inspiration and healing very helpful!

A. Websites

1. Rick Broniec's Website: www.vibrantrelationshipsguy.com
2. The ManKind Project: www.mankindproject.org
3. Re-Evaluation Counselling: www.rc.org
4. 12-Step work: www.aa.org
5. Laurie Ingraham's work: Addictive Relationships Center in Brookfield, Wisconsin.
6. Self-Realization Fellowship: www.yogananda-srf.org/
7. Wildquest – The Human-Dolphin Connection: www.wildquest.com
8. VISIONS, Inc.: www.visions-inc.org

B. Books

Native American Stories and Myths

9. *History, Myths and Sacred Formulas of the Cherokees*, James Mooney, Bright Mountain Books, 1992.
14. *Medicine Cards: The Discovery of Power Through the Ways of Animals*, Jamie Sams and David Carson, Bear and Company, Santa Fe, NM, 1988.
15. *Animal-Speak: The Spiritual & Magical Powers of Creatures Great and Small*, Ted Andrews, Llewellyn Worldwide, Minneapolis, MN, 1993.

16. *Grandfather Stories of the Navajos*, Sydney M. Callaway and Gary Witherspooon, Rough Rock Press, AZ.
17. *The Four Agreements*, Don Miguel Ruiz, Amber Allen Publishing, San Rafael, CA, 1999.

Multicultural Awareness
18. Race Manners for the 21st Century, Bruce A. Jacobs, Arcade Publishing, 2006.
19. Uprooting Racism: How White People Can Work for Racial Justice, Paul Kivel, New Society Publishers, 2002.
20. Teaching Diversity and Social Justice, Maurianne Adams, Lee Ann Bell, Pat Griffin, Routledge, 1997.

Leadership and Healing
21. *Fierce Leadership*, Susan Scott, Crown Business, 2009.
22. *Daring Greatly*, Brene Brown, PhD, Gotham Books, 2012.
23. *Leadership from the Inside Out*, Kevin Cashman, Berrit-Koehler Publishing, 2008.
24. *Change the World*, Robert E. Quinn, John Wiley & Sons, 2000.
25. *Emotional Intelligence*, Daniel Goleman, Bantam, 1995.
26. *A New Earth: Awakening to Your Life's Purpose*, Eckart Tolle, Penguin Group, 2005.
27. *Focus on the Good Stuff*, Mike Robbins, John Wiley & Sons, 2007.
28. *Be Yourself: Everyone Else is Already Taken*, Mike Robbins, Jossey-Bass, 2009.
29. *Nothing Changes Until You Do*, Mike Robbins, Hay House, 2014.

Family Constellation Therapy

30. *The Healing of Individuals, Families & Nations*, John L. Payne, Findhorn Press, 2007.
31. *Family Constellation: Its Effects on Personality and Social Behavior*, 4th Edition, Walter Toman, PhD, Springer Publishing, 1961.
32. *Multigenerational Family Therapy*, David S. Freeman, Taylor & Francis, 1991.
33. *Family Constellations: A Practical Guide to Uncovering the Origins of Family Conflict*, Joy Manne, PhD, North Atlantic Books, 2009.
34. *Love's Hidden Symmetry: What Makes Love Work in Relationships*, Bert Hellinger, Zeig, Tucker & Theisen, 1998.

Made in the USA
San Bernardino, CA
10 April 2015